TOWARD ONE WORLD:
THE LIFE OF WENDELL WILLKIE

TOWARD ONE WORLD:

The Life of

WENDELL

WILLKIE

by BILL SEVERN

IVES WASHBURN, INC. · NEW YORK

TOWARD ONE WORLD:
THE LIFE OF WENDELL WILLKIE

COPYRIGHT © 1967 BY BILL SEVERN

LIBRARY OF CONGRESS CATALOG CARD NUMBER: 67-22010

MANUFACTURED IN THE UNITED STATES OF AMERICA

TOWARD ONE WORLD:
THE LIFE OF WENDELL WILLKIE

Chapter One

A QUARTER of a million people crowded into the small central-Indiana town of Elwood on August 17, 1940, to listen to a man who had been almost unknown to most Americans two years before. A lifelong Democrat, he was to be for a brief time the leader of the Republican party. He had never been elected to any public office and never would be, but by his sheer ability and force of character he would have enormous influence upon the nation during a decisive period of history.

Wendell Willkie had been a wealthy corporation president, but also a fighting liberal; a spokesman for big business, but also a supporter of many of the social reforms of the New Deal. A unique individual, with a bold sense of dramatic action that captured public attention and focused it upon the important decisions that had to be made in a time of crisis for democracy, he challenged blind tradition wherever he found it and opened people's minds to a broader view of both America and the world.

On that sweltering August day in 1940, he hoped to be the next President of the United States and as thousands ate hot

1

dogs and waved Willkie banners in a park that had once
been a meadow through which he drove a neighbor's cow as
a daily chore to earn pocket money as a boy, he was remembering his beginnings in Elwood. Removing his flat straw hat
to run his hand through his tousled hair, he wiped the
perspiration from his face, and in the hoarse, urgent voice all
America would come to know he formally accepted the
Republican party's nomination.

"There is a special reason why I have come back to Elwood, Indiana, to make this acceptance speech," he said. "I
have an engagement to keep in this town. It was made a long
time ago by a young man I knew well. This young man was
born and raised in Elwood. As I look back upon him, I
realize he had plenty of faults. But he also had steadfast
convictions. He was devoted to the ideal of individual
liberty. He hated all special privileges and forms of oppres-
sion." He went on:

> In former days, America was described as a country in which
> any young man might become President. The thousands of
> my fellow townsmen standing hereabout know how distant
> seemed that opportunity to me thirty years ago. . . . I want to
> say in all humility—this boy I knew started like you, without
> money or position, but America gave him the opportunity for a
> career.
>
> I have more reason than most of you to feel strongly about
> this because the United States gave to my family their first
> chance for a free life. The ancestors of both my father and my
> mother, like the ancestors of millions of Americans, lived in
> Central Europe. Their opportunities were restricted by dis-
> criminatory laws and class distinctions. . . .

As he spoke, there must have been in his mind the stories he
had heard so often about his adventurous grandfather,
Joseph William Willeke, the coppersmith of Aschersleben in
Saxony who had joined the liberals trying to throw off

2

Austrian military domination in the German revolution of 1848. When the revolution failed and military forces took control, Grandfather Willeke had many disputes with the strutting officers who imposed authority. After his second child, Herman Francis, was born in 1857, he decided he could no longer live in a land that lacked personal freedom and he set out the next year to find a home in America. Eventually he located a farm ten miles south of Fort Wayne, Indiana, and in 1861 returned to Germany long enough to get his wife and family and bring them to the United States.

Although Fort Wayne itself had become a city, the farm was still frontier country where the last of the Indian raids had threatened settlers not many years before. As young Herman Willeke grew, he helped his father clear the land, fell trees, and plow and seed the farm, although his father was not as good a farmer as he had been a coppersmith. But from him Herman learned a love of reading and a hunger for education.

He managed to get all the schooling available, even though the nearest school meant a four-mile daily walk and the term lasted only four months a year. With his father's farm hardly prospering, and with seven brothers and sisters in the family, there was no money for college so Herman dug ditches and worked as a harvest hand until he finally saved a little more than a hundred dollars, enough in those days for a year's tuition, books, board and lodging at Valparaiso College. The college registrar misspelled the German name Willeke as Willkie, and Herman decided that was easier for most people so he kept it that way. After a year at Valparaiso he was able to get a job as a county school teacher and to enter Fort Wayne College, closer to home. Alternating between teaching jobs and college study, he worked his way through to graduate with high honors in 1884.

The year he graduated, Herman Willkie became superin-

3

tendent of schools at Milford, Indiana, where he met and fell in love with one of his grammar school teachers, Henrietta Trisch. Both her parents, like his, had come from Germany in search of freedom.

Her father, Lewis Trisch, had been brought to Baltimore as a year-old baby after the Trischs fled from Hessen-Darmstadt, where her grandfather had been a wagon maker, following the collapse of the revolution of 1829. Henrietta's mother, Julia von Hessen-Lois, had escaped from her aristocratic home in Hamburg minutes before police arrived to seize and jail her family for speaking out against the government, and Julia had fled to England and then worked her passage to America as a lady's maid.

Henrietta's mother and father had met and married in Warsaw, Indiana, where Lewis Trisch was a frontier blacksmith, had adventured farther west together by stagecoach to Fort Dodge, Kansas, to run a general store, but had been driven out of "Bleeding Kansas" by pre-Civil War rioters who threatened to lynch them for being against slavery. Having fled from Germany because of one form of intolerance and from Kansas because of another, Henrietta's parents returned to their former home in Warsaw, Indiana, where her father made wagons for the Union Army during the Civil War, and edited the local newspaper until his death in 1873. Her mother then became a temperance lecturer and Presbyterian lay preacher who rode horseback over the area, holding revival meetings as "Mother Trisch." Henrietta's sister Jennie was one of Indiana's first woman doctors.

When Henrietta Trisch fell in love with Herman Willkie, her new school superintendent at Milford, she was beginning her first job, having just received her teaching diploma from Terre Haute Normal School. Herman soon learned of a better teaching position at Lagro, Indiana, and they decided to get married and go there together. The ceremony was

4

performed in the parlor of Fort Wayne College by its
president, Doctor Yokum, and on the Christmas day that
ended their first year in Lagro the Willkies' first daughter,
Julia, was born, and two years later their first son, Robert.

Meanwhile, Herman had been offered a chance to take
over the school system in Elwood, a town that had become
the talk of all Indiana. A great discovery of natural gas had
turned the tiny farming hamlet into a small industrial city
almost overnight. Boosters were glibly predicting that Elwood, at the center of the new field, was on its way toward
becoming a great metropolis of the Midwest, and Herman
saw it as the place of the future for himself and his young
family.

"The gas reservoir beneath us is beyond the scope of
computation," a town booklet boasted. In the cornfields
around Elwood uncapped wells burned with columns of
flame that shot two hundred feet into the air. Great gas
candelabra lighted Elwood's streets and burned day and
night because it seemed not worth the trouble or expense to
turn them off when daylight came. Any family could have all
the gas needed to heat a home, cook, and keep the lights
blazing for eighty-five cents a month. Population had jumped
three hundred per cent, and that was only the beginning.

Money and industry flooded into the village on Duck
Creek, forty miles from Indianapolis, attracted by the seemingly limitless supply of clean, cheap fuel. Manufacturers
built factories to make plate glass, lamp chimneys, boilers,
engines, and furniture. Workers came by the hundreds to
take jobs and run the swelling business of the booming town.
Streets were mostly unpaved, sidewalks were wooden, indoor plumbing and bathtubs were rarities, but Elwood had a
fine hotel, a railroad depot and an opera house, and spreading streets of stores.

It was into that prospering community, bursting at its

5

seams, that Herman Willkie came in 1888 to take charge of the schools, but the task at first almost floored him. The four rooms just added to the brick schoolhouse couldn't begin to hold the town's new children, and he found that classes had never been graded at all and that pupils were simply herded together by age and size rather than by ability. He planned and set up graded classes and then because there was no high school of any kind organized that, and taught algebra, arithmetic and Latin himself, with one assistant for all the other subjects.

He was a well-liked schoolmaster, but apparently a strict one, privately nicknamed by some of his pupils, "Hellfire Willkie." But the nickname might have come as much from the adult Sunday school class he taught for years at the Methodist church, where Henrietta taught the children's classes. Herman's father had been a devout Catholic, as most of his brothers and sisters were, but in his teens he had joined his mother's Methodist faith. The Willkies, from the time they arrived, were among the leaders of Elwood's progressive middle class. In addition to being a pillar of the church, Herman headed a literary circle, organized a group to study University of Chicago extension courses, was a staunch Democrat active in politics, and a frequent public speaker.

A brawny six-footer, he did some of the carpentry himself on their first home. Quick to realize the demand for housing by workers who came to the new industries, he started building small homes for them, soon pyramided his profits, and eventually put up more than two hundred little houses. Some he rented and others he sold on time payments for which he endorsed the notes. He was able to invest in a brick yard, a sawmill, a canning factory and other enterprises, did well during the first boom years, and before long

6

announced plans for a Willkie Block of stores and offices in Elwood's business section.

With all its growing industries, gas leases and rapid real estate turnover, Elwood needed more lawyers. The law had always interested Herman, and he decided it offered a better future than teaching school, so he added the study of law to his other activities. No college law degree was necessary in those days,—only the proper character references and a stiff oral examination by a Circuit Court judge. Henrietta spent hours reading law with him, acting as his coach and prompter, and with her help he taught himself, brilliantly passed the examination and was admitted to the Indiana bar September 25, 1890. He immediately gave up his position as school superintendent to start his new profession. Five days after he became a lawyer, he and Henrietta celebrated the birth of their third child, christened Herman Frederick, but always known to the family as Fred.

The growing Willkie family moved into a bigger house and later to a still larger one, all on the same street of downtown Elwood. Herman became a crusading lawyer, a battler for the workers and the little people rather than for wealthy clients, seldom happy unless he was fighting some cause for the underdog, often at the sacrifice of large fees. But among his first law clients was a group of bankers, and through them Elwood came into its greatest boom.

For years England had a near-monopoly on the manufacture of tinplate, and although some was made in the United States, no practical way had been found to produce it at low cost. But when the tariff on English tinplate was doubled, an American financial group became interested in the problem and was impressed by Elwood's cheap natural gas supply and the town's geographical location between the source of iron in Pittsburgh and the tin of South Dakota's Black Hills.

Elwood offered to give the financial combine a fourteen-acre farm near a gas well called the Vesuvius as the site for a plant. The bankers hired Willkie as a lawyer to investigate the town's real estate offer. His report helped sway the decision to build the first big tinplate factory in the United States in Elwood, one that would draw in hundreds of additional workers as it eventually became the center of a huge complex of mills.

Elwood was riding a new wave of prosperity as construction began. Almost every week there was something for the town to celebrate, the opening of an electricity plant, a municipal water plant, a telephone exchange. But the Willkies had a more private event to celebrate on February 18, 1892, the birth of their fourth child, another son, named Lewis Wendell, but soon better known as Wendell or Wen.

The town had no way of guessing he would someday become Elwood's most famous native son, and the really big news that day was that when the tinplate plant was dedicated there would be a gala ceremony at the opera house that would bring to Elwood a man being talked of as a possible future President of the United States, Governor William McKinley of Ohio.

People came from all over Indiana on September 13, 1892, to attend the tinplant dedication and there were dignitaries from nearby states, leaders of industry, frock-coated financiers from New York and Boston. There were bands and a parade, and the huge crowd finally backed up all along the railroad tracks and as far as the street where the Willkies lived. Wendell was far too young to understand the tumult around him. Yet among his first conscious impressions may have been the roar of the crowd.

As William McKinley stepped to the balcony of the opera house to make his speech, he stood at a table that would be

8

used again in 1940 in the campaign headquarters at Elwood when Wendell Willkie also ran for President. But for the infant just born into that roaring town, 1940 was still forty-eight years away.

Chapter Two

WENDELL WILLKIE was never a farm boy. The town in which he grew served surrounding farms, but his childhood years were closer to the factory than the plow. Elwood was a wide-open, rip-roaring little city, as rough in some of its ways as any boomtown of the Western frontier. Wages were high, spending was free, and saloons and gambling halls flourished.

Crop reports still made front-page news in local papers, but so did reports of violence. There were quiet streets of tall oaks and maples, and also noisy clusters of dingy slums. It was a place of open fields where a boy could run barefoot and the fenced-in yards of smoke-belching factories. Creaking wagons were chased by clanging street cars. Farmers who crowded into Elwood on Saturday nights mingled with city-bred glass workers from Pittsburgh, factory hands from the North and West, and Welshmen imported from their foreign homeland to bring special skills to the tinplate plant. It was a town where a boy learned early to fight for what he wanted and also learned that the world was made of many kinds of people who lived lives different from his own.

The town's first memory of Wendell was as a "stubby little

fellow" who had to reach high for the hand his father held down to him, a toddler so interested in everything around him that he was forever stumbling on the uneven walks. The family finances also became uneven the year after he was born when Herman Willkie was hard hit by the panic of 1893, and instead of getting rich found himself struggling to keep from going bankrupt, so Wendell was anything but a pampered boy, although the Willkies were far from being poverty-stricken.

By Elwood's standards they were considered the most unconventional family in town, close in their affections but each an individual and often stubbornly so. It was said of them that they would rather argue than eat. Readers, talkers, thinkers, they carried on endless family debates over philosophy, science, politics, or whatever subject aroused them at the moment.

Wendell's mother had a reputation for keeping a spotlessly clean house, making clothes from patterns she designed herself, putting up hundreds of quarts of fruits and jellies, and baking the family's bread. But she also was plainly bored by the small routine household tasks that were the whole life of most of her women neighbors. Friends said that she seemed determined to disprove the German tradition that a woman's world began and ended in family, children, and church. With a forceful character, a strong will, and a driving energy of body and mind, she had a competitive spirit that constantly demanded some new challenge. From herself, she demanded perfection in everything she did, and she expected no less from others.

Some of Wendell's boyhood friends adored Henrietta Willkie while others remembered her as cold and strict. Neighborhood children were given the run of the house and she could be brightly entertaining with those she liked, as she was with people of any age when they interested her,

11

but she made no pretense of seeking affection, and displays of sentiment embarrassed her. Far from being a possessive mother, she was more tolerant than most, but when she did issue a command there was no appeal from her decision. Casual about their food and clothing, she let the boys run barefoot from spring to fall and provided them with hearty meals, but of a kind that wasted little of her time to prepare.

As intense about her hobbies as she was about everything else she did, Wendell's mother played the piano, sang, painted delicate pictures on china, won prizes for embroidery, did intricate needlework, and taught herself French and Spanish. All her energy went into whatever challenged her at the moment, but when she conquered it she lost interest.

Wendell and his brothers loved and respected their mother, but they worshipped their father. A kind-hearted, affectionate, tender man, he took far more interest in his children than most fathers did in those days. When Wendell was a baby, it usually was his father who hurried into the room to comfort him if he cried at night, who took him in his arms to carry him about the house, and who put him into his carriage to take him out for an airing. Herman Willkie's whole pride was in his children, and he devoted himself to them.

He usually woke them in the mornings by quoting some proverb. "Time to get up," he would call from the doorway. "'Shall I let the ants and the bees be wise while I my moments waste?'" Wendell and the others learned to make a game of answering with some other quotation and that would start a round of jokes and laughter that carried them all to the breakfast table. At breakfast, lunch, and dinner, the table was a family forum, with Wendell's mother and father leading the talk on their own adult level, but with the children allowed a full say on any subject that came up.

12

Their father encouraged them to defend their views, no matter how childish their opinions might be. He taught them to ask questions, to seek truth, to accept nobody's answers as final, and to see that all problems had many sides.

Wendell knew about books before he knew what they were. They were among the first things his baby eyes focused upon beyond his crib. His mother usually had one under her arm when she kissed him good-night and his father often read from an open book as he pushed Wendell's carriage or carried him about the house on his hip. The house overflowed with books, on shelves and tables and in stacks that towered up from the floors, some six thousand of them in the Willkie home at a time when most neighbors had only a few or at most a few dozen. His father and mother later helped found the town library and led the drive to raise funds for it, but it was years before the public library had as many books as the Willkies owned.

"When your grandfather first came to Fort Wayne it was wilderness and there were few belongings the pioneers could bring with them," Wendell's father once told him. "Many were able to bring just one book and that book, whatever it was, became a symbol of all the culture they had been forced to leave behind. But with my generation life became easier. So when we had a little extra money we bought more books." He swept his arm toward all the books in the room. "Now they are yours."

While his mother painted in the evenings or busied herself with one of her hobbies, his father read aloud to the family. He had learned to use his voice well, both as a lawyer and public speaker, and was able to bring tales of adventure, deeds of history, the sweeping passages of poetry and plays vividly alive. Long before Wendell started school he had learned to read for himself, and all the books were his to ex-

13

plore, with none ever forbidden to him simply because he was too young.

But against the intellectual background of his home, the booming factory town offered a boy adventures of a rougher kind, and he grew as much in the town as in the book-filled house. As soon as he was old enough to join his brothers Bob and Fred at play, there was hardly a daylight hour he spent indoors. The boys were given the freedom to roam the town as they pleased, with nobody to suggest how they should keep themselves amused. Wendell's neighborhood pals included the four McCarel boys whose father worked at the tin-plate mill, the Cox youngsters whose father was a printer, and the Silvys, sons of a teamster. With them he learned to explore trash heaps to search for interesting treasures, to beg grocers for empty wooden boxes and saloon keepers for discarded barrels, and from such things the boys made sleds and wagons, huts and kites. Once they discovered a big stack of rotted planks that had been taken up from the sidewalks, and Wendell helped drag the boards home one at a time to try to build a roller coaster like the one at the fair grounds.

He became an expert at marbles and in winter a good skater and snowball maker. When there was nothing to build and nothing new to explore in town, there was tag to play, trees to climb, fences to walk the tops of, hikes to take. In summer there was the swimming hole at Duck Creek or, if that had run dry, they could walk south of town for a dip in the mudhole back of one of the factories. A husky boy, vocal in his opinions, Wendell soon learned to back them with his fists. He suffered thumps and bruises and took a good share of beatings that left his knees and elbows skinned, but the only complaint his older brothers had was that he never knew when he was licked and they sometimes had to drag him, still kicking and swinging, from brawls with boys twice his size.

Wendell and his brothers dropped whatever they were doing when Grandfather Willkie came to Elwood on one of his visits from his home in Fort Wayne, bringing special treats of candy, cheese, and highly-spiced sausages, and willing to be coaxed into telling the tales they begged to hear of his adventures when the Willkies first came to pioneer Indiana.

On Decoration Day there was the parade of the veterans of the Union Army and the military music of the Tin Plate Band, and on the Fourth of July there was patriotic speechmaking that went on for hours while the boys, as good sons of a good Democrat, cheered in the right places. Christmas meant a trip to the woods to cut a tree, the family ritual of lighting the candles, fireplace stockings filled with nuts and fruit, and best of all the year's one store-bought toy or special gift that rewarded months of eager hope and good behavior. Christmas Day, 1896, brought particular joy to the Willkies because that was when Wendell's brother Edward was born.

After Edward's birth, Wendell's mother decided she also would become a lawyer and help his father in the legal practice that was growing too big for him to handle alone. Helping him study law had already taught her much of what she needed to know and although some of the male members of the bar were shocked by the thought of admitting a female to their ranks, she overcame their resistance, passed her examination, and in 1897 became one of Indiana's first woman lawyers. She joined Wendell's father in the firm that became Willkie & Willkie and began putting in full days and many nights handling the overflow legal business. Once she and Herman opposed each other as lawyers for contest-

15

ing parties in a suit and she won the case, much to her husband's own delight.

Since her law work took her away from home during the day, she hired a housekeeper, and Wendell's older sister Julia, twelve by then, pitched in to help. Forced to be self-reliant, the boys apparently managed pretty well for themselves although some disapproving neighbors spoke of them as the "wild Willkie kids." But however much mischief they might get into during the day, there was no letdown in family discipline in the evenings. They had to be subdued, washed, in clean clothes, and with their hair combed, before they could take their places at the supper table.

Wendell disliked Sundays because he had to wear shoes all day instead of going barefoot and because his mother dressed him up in what he considered sissy clothes. There was Sunday School in the morning, then church services, and finally family readings from the Bible. But though the Willkies were strict Methodists who frowned upon such things as card playing, liquor, and dancing, they were tolerant toward all beliefs, even to the point of including the lectures of agnostic Robert Ingersoll in their family readings.

Barefoot days ended for Wendell in 1899 when he started school at the age of seven and had to wear shoes not only on Sunday but every day. His mother insisted, and his father agreed since he felt school was a privilege his son should learn to prize with respect. As former school teachers themselves, both his parents were ambitious for him to do well. Elwood's new Central School, just opened that year, housed both grade and high school classes in a fort-like red brick building with a bell tower atop. On an arch above the entrance, spelled out in swirling stone letters crossed by decorative stars and bars, was the slogan *The Hope of Our Country*, which amused the students because the stonecutter had chiseled the letter "N" backwards. Wendell's hardest first lesson was learning that he couldn't shout in class and had to curb his restless wandering and stay put at his small desk, bolted into a row with the others.

It was a big year in his life. His sister Charlotte, the last of the six Willkie children, was born in October; the town was aroused to patriotic fervor by parades and bands and waving flags as victorious soldiers began returning from the Spanish-American War; and his family was planning to build a new home on another block of the street where they now lived. His mother had found the design for the house in the pages of a women's magazine. It was to be three stories high, with a wide front porch, a steep gabled roof, and outside walls of scalloped green shingles.

Wendell spent most of his spare time watching the builders at work and doing what they would let a boy do. Downstairs there was a parlor with big bay windows, a music room on the other side, and a large walnut-beamed dining room that ran the width of the house at the rear. There was a red brick fireplace in that and also a rope-pulled dumbwaiter to bring things up from the kitchen below. In the kitchen, where the Willkies would eat most of their meals when they didn't have company, was another great fireplace. A solid oak staircase with strong bannisters he immediately tried to slide down led to the second floor where bookshelves in the circular library rose to the ceiling. Next to that was a guest room, a smaller room for sister Julia and baby Charlotte, and a bedroom at the back for his mother and father. The four boys would have a large bedroom over the parlor, with beds for Bob and Ed at one end, and for Fred and Wendell at the other, and he would be able to look from his bed through a window with stained glass panels at the sides that sparkled bright pink and blue when the sun shone through.

17

The twentieth century was a half-year old in June, 1900, when Wendell and his family moved into the new house. Neighborhood youngsters enjoyed the run of the place and its big grape-arbored yard, and there was hardly an afternoon when he and his brothers and sisters didn't have up to a dozen friends around. On rainy days they had the whole attic to themselves for a playroom. They built a soap-box stage and put on free-style versions of Shakespeare's plays, and others they wrote themselves around stories from books they had read, and when Wendell couldn't remember his lines he made them up as he went along.

But he still liked to roam the town and hike into the nearby countryside when the weather was good. One Saturday he and his brother Bob and his pal, Earl McCarel, hiked to the nearby town of Dundee, carrying their food with them and stopping to swim in a creek on the way. They grew weary walking back and hitched a ride on a horse-drawn rig built to carry long lengths of gas pipe. Astride a fifty-foot wooden beam that connected the back and front sets of wheels, Wendell fell asleep with the slow jogging, lost his balance and toppled from the rig. His leg was crushed under the wheels and so badly cut he had the scar the rest of his life.

Old enough by then to take in some of the talk of politics that went on at home, he loyally sided with his father and boyishly rated Democrats as the good guys and Republicans as the bad guys, which made William Jennings Bryan a hero and William McKinley a villain. His unquestioning young faith in Democrats and his interest in the presidential campaign of 1900 took an upward leap when he learned that Bryan was coming right to his own house to visit his father.

Herman Willkie was Elwood's Democratic leader, and he and Bryan also were personal friends from working together on Sunday school conferences so the famed orator took an

18

hour off to spend at the Willkie home as he came through Indiana at the end of his hard and for-the-second-time unsuccessful presidential campaign against McKinley. Bryan must have been a weary man, under all the pressures of the coming election, but he was patient and friendly with the Willkie boys. Wendell never forgot his expressive face and deep brown eyes or the compelling voice that hushed all other conversation in the Willkie living room. After meeting him that night, shaking the hand of the man he thought should be President, he found it hard to understand the nation's decision in November when the voters chose McKinley again instead of Bryan.

Aside from politics, Wendell's father was busier than ever before, buying real estate again, mortgaging it and buying more, trying to recoup his earlier losses. He also insisted that the boys work at spare-time jobs as soon as they were big enough, not only to teach them thrift and industry but so they would learn the satisfaction of earning for themselves. Wendell's first job, handed down to him by his brother Fred, was driving a cow owned by Mrs. De Hority from her barn to a pasture at the edge of town. He had to be up at six in the morning to fetch the cow before he went to school, and on some sleepy mornings when he grew tired of walking, he rode the beast. Later he and Fred delivered advertising handbills to every home in town for two dollars a thousand. At other times, he delivered newspapers, sorted good potatoes from bad for a wholesale grocer, and was paid twenty-five cents a bucket by junkman Abe Levi for grading nails and tacks gathered up in floor sweepings at a box factory.

But Elwood's brief period of prosperity was running out. The underground gas, expected to flow forever, had been extravagantly wasted, tapped by too many pipelines, sent by pumping stations to distant cities with little thought of conservation. As the reserve pressure fell, water crept into some

19

of the wells and the supply became undependable. The collapse came over a period of several years, but on a cold January morning in 1903, the Willkies awoke to discover that their side of town had no gas for light or heat.

They huddled around the kitchen fireplace, stuffed with newspapers, and finally broke up old furniture to burn for warmth. As other failures came, some factories turned to the use of coal but others with heavy investment in gas equipment were unable to convert. With the cheap natural fuel dwindling, small plants and then larger ones closed down. The big tinplate mill stayed in operation and some others struggled along for a time but the town's economic life, built on the promise of gas, came to a standstill. There was nothing left in Elwood to attract new capital or industry. Hundreds of workers were forced out of their jobs and gave up their homes to head for other places. Parts of Elwood resembled a ghost town, and the dream of becoming a great metropolis was over. It would never again be a city as big as it was.

Wendell's father was left holding mortgages on homes workers had deserted, on land nobody wanted to buy, investments in businesses that showed no profit. For several years things were so bad he was in a constant struggle with the banks to keep them from foreclosing on everything he had. He avoided that, but the lasting burden of debt was so heavy he spent a good part of his life working out from under it. During the rest of Wendell's boyhood the family had financial ups and downs.

But if Elwood had lost its dream, Wendell hadn't yet found his ambition. He had become a young man of fourteen in 1906 when he left the classroom to cross the hall and enter high school. But beyond that, he had no idea where he wanted to go.

Chapter Three

D<small>URING</small> most of his life Wendell Willkie had done pretty much as he pleased, and he rebelled against the strict new discipline of high school. He was bored by classroom routine, uninspired by his teachers, found his textbooks dull, and seemed to resent the whole process of being forced to learn by rote instead of being allowed to think for himself. Tough, aggressive, determined to assert himself as an individual, he argued with his teachers, disputed the rules, and started out as anything but a prize student.

He had poor marks in Latin, ancient history and botany and only average grades in algebra and composition for his first half-year, and by the end of the year he was poor in all subjects and almost failed in botany. Because he had read so much on his own, he probably was far beyond his schoolmates in general knowledge, but he apparently seldom opened a textbook if he could avoid it. His teachers told his father he had a good mind but just wouldn't apply himself.

Lanky, tall, and still growing, his tousled hair seldom combed, he wore sloppy turtleneck sweaters, sprawled when he sat, and looked ready to run when he walked, and was physically and mentally restless. In defiance of a school rule for proper dress, he appeared one morning with his trousers rolled up to display a green stocking on one foot and a red stocking on the other, and with frilly feminine garters of contrasting colors on his shirtsleeves.

With some of his friends, he formed a secret club complete with signs, codes, and passwords that met in the basement of the Willkie home where he devised a makeshift gymnasium. But the members seemed more devoted to planning adventures than indoor sports. In one of their pranks, he led a night raid on the school's physiology classroom to kidnap a skeleton he and his pals dismembered and hung from the branches of a tree.

Yet he did worry privately about his low marks, and he was far from lazy in holding down an after-school job driving a horse-drawn delivery wagon for one of Elwood's bakers. He also put in some hard work helping his father move a number of the small houses that had been built for factory workers and left deserted when the gas boom collapsed. His father had managed to salvage some of his investment by selling the houses to nearby farmers for use as barns and storage sheds, and Wendell helped jack them up on wheels and drove one of the teams that hauled them out to the farms.

When summer came, he and a friend, George De Hority, hopefully planned to ride their bicycles halfway across the country to Washington to visit the nation's capital. But George's parents as well as Wendell's felt the boys were more in need of strict discipline and extra school work, so they decided to send them off together to the Culver Military Academy summer camp in Northern Indiana. Wendell hated every minute of it. He was homesick and miserably unhappy and the military discipline of the Academy went against everything in his nature. Reluctantly he agreed to wear the school's uniform of a sailor suit and flat-topped hat with the name Culver on its black ribbon band, but he refused to accept the traditional hazing by older students without a fight, and as a result suffered more of it than most newcomers.

He did learn to row a boat and to enjoy sailing on Lake Maxinkuckee, and his swimming became easy and graceful. The daily drilling and marching in formation helped correct his posture, and although he detested the stern classroom regimen and the specified no-nonsense study periods, he finished the summer at Culver with much better study habits.

But when the session was over, he was glad to escape and join his family for a brief vacation at Lake Barbee, an Indiana resort where the Willkies had a small cottage. Inspired by his newly-gained knowledge of boats, Wendell convinced his nine-year-old brother Ed they should follow the example set centuries before by French explorer La Salle and make their way to the Mississippi by water. Their father agreed to let them try, and the boys packed canned food, eggs, and a tent aboard a small rowboat and set out at dawn on the route of connecting waterways they had mapped. After three days of rough going, they had aching backs and blistered hands, bad cases of sunburn, and were almost too exhausted to eat. They tied up the boat and beat their way through a swampy woods to reach a road where they discovered that all their labored rowing had taken them only twenty miles from the cottage where they had started. Discouraged, they quit the adventure, abandoned the boat, and hitch-hiked back to Lake Barbee.

That fall Wendell tried out for football and made the Elwood High School team. He also gained a close new friend in Paul Harmon, a newcomer to Elwood, and he began to take an interest in girls. One of the first girls Wendell tried to date turned him down because her mother objected to letting her go out with "one of those wild Willkie boys," but others remembered him in later years as a well-behaved young man. They enjoyed sledding parties, hay rides, and informal evenings at the Willkie home where a group would gather around the piano to sing and have ice cream afterwards. Dancing was not permitted, and he never did learn to dance well although he tried to learn after he was in college.

When the Willkie boys started dating, their father said he wouldn't set any strict rule about what time they had to be home but that they mustn't get into the habit of making up in the daytime for the sleep they lost at night. "If you're home at the normal time, you may sleep in the morning until the time you usually get up," he said, "but if you don't get in until midnight then I'll see to it that you get up at dawn. Any time you wander in at two in the morning, I promise to rout you out of bed at four. I may lose my own sleep, but you can count on it that you'll also lose yours."

On nights when they had no dates, Wendell and his pals might hang around "Doc" Hinshaw's drugstore or gather somewhere for a bull session. They decided one night to advertise their class by climbing a dangerously high steel ladder to the top of a towering gas tank behind an abandoned factory, rigging a rope to let themselves down over the side, and using a can of bright yellow paint to emblazon *E.H.S.* '10 in dripping big strokes for the whole town to see. It was the talk of Elwood for days, and while authorities tried to discover who had done it, the boys added to the uproar by going out another night and marking up the walks around the school with their class numerals. The principal called all the likely suspects into his office and demanded the truth. "I want each of you who painted on those walks to admit it," he said. Wendell held out until he was directly challenged

24

and then answered: "We didn't paint the walks. We used shoe polish."

But during his second year in high school he began to lose interest in such things and was inspired to improve his marks and get something from his education. The inspiration came from two sources, a teacher who helped awaken his mind and change his whole attitude toward learning, and a girl with whom he fell in love.

The teacher was Philip Carleton Bing, who had come to Elwood to teach English fresh from his own studies at the University of Chicago. Tall, red-haired, with a sharp sense of humor, driving intellectual energy, and little regard for conventional teaching methods, he was still in his early twenties and eager to give all of himself to the profession he had chosen as the best any man could follow. Most of his students thought of him as a friend, called him "Pat," and enjoyed his company in school and out. They invited him to their homes, gathered at his place in the evenings to debate things that had come up in class, and welcomed him into all their activities.

Bing firmly believed that the greatest thing he could teach his students was to think for themselves. He provoked them to challenge his opinions, question everything he said, and to look up the answers and prove him wrong if they could. They were encouraged to argue, to speak out, to bring up any subject that touched upon what they were studying, and the more controversial the better. Often they wandered far away from English lessons, but they did read good books and thought deeply about them in seeking the knowledge he led them to discover, and they also learned that the exchange of ideas could be exciting and that learning could be fun.

Paul Harmon suggested as a joke in class one day that there wasn't much difference between the pronunciation

25

of "liar" and "lawyer" and that maybe the two words meant the same thing. Wendell jumped into the discussion and delivered an impromptu speech in defense of his father's profession. Delighted by his response, Bing began to introduce other subjects that would challenge him to speak. For Wendell, brought up on family debates, Bing's class was like coming home. Under Bing's influence, he became aware of the pleasure of using his mind, eager to study, and his interest carried over into other classes. Most of his grades became good and then excellent. He wanted Bing's approval and sought his admiration with an enthusiasm that was almost hero worship.

There were times when Wendell's new-found pride in scholarship took a fall. He once got the wrong spot while dramatically reciting a speech from Shakespeare's *As You Like It* and instead of saying, "And first the infant, muling and puking in the nurse's arms . . ." he said, "And first the infant, muling and puking in the nurse's eye." The class roared, and after a moment's embarrassment he joined in the laughter. Another time, as captain of a boys' team in a debate against a team led by girls, he expected an easy victory. But the girls, determined to show him up, worked for days digging out their arguments. Wendell was stunned when the judges declared the girls had won, and although he managed to offer his congratulations, his classmates said that for once in his life he was almost speechless.

Despite his hero worship of Bing, he was no teacher's pet. But as good personal friends as well as teacher and student, when Wendell's interest in one of the girls in class became obvious, Bing decided to help them become better acquainted.

She was Gwyneth Harry, a bright and very pretty dark-haired girl, two years younger than Wendell was at sixteen but only half a year behind him in her studies. Bing considered Wendell and Gwyneth the most brilliant of his students and approved the growing friendship as good for both of them. He knew the Harry family well and went to the Episcopal church they attended, where Gwyneth sang in the choir, so he suggested to Wendell that he might want to come along to the services some Sunday and be properly introduced. Wendell eagerly accepted, and they all walked home together after church.

The Harrys were from Wales, and Gwyneth's father had come to Elwood to help introduce Welsh manufacturing skills into the town's tinplate industry. They were among Elwood's solidly conservative and fairly well-to-do middle class. Gwyneth's home, like his, was filled with well-read books and her parents were cultured, educated, and proud of their British heritage. He and Bing were invited to stay for luncheon, and spent most of the afternoon with the Harrys. After that, the walks home from church, and Sundays spent with Gwyneth and her family became a regular thing and Wendell needed no more encouragement from his teacher. He fell romantically and completely in love, and Gwyneth became the center of his life, of his hopes and ambitions, and of a devotion that lasted for years.

Because of her, he joined the Episcopal church and in addition to finding a new interest in religion gave up some of his spare time to mow the church lawn and act as unpaid janitor, and later became a lay reader at services. Gwyneth strengthened his new attitude toward school and his seriousness toward the future. She also tried to improve his grooming and his manners. Yet even with her he frequently rebelled against what he considered meaningless conformity to things that seemed to him totally unimportant. He wore good clothes but remained unconcerned about whether his trousers were pressed, his tie was straight, or a button was missing from his jacket. She objected to his habit of munch-

27

ing apples as they walked together, but he went right on devouring them, sometimes core and all. Most of all he still liked to argue about anything and everything and he often deliberately took the opposite side of a question to tease her with outrageous statements just for the fun of arguing.

When summer came in 1908, Wendell was determined to hold down a man's job during the months he was free from school; and by claiming to be a year older than he was, he talked one of the bosses at the tinplate factory into hiring him to work with a "hot mill" crew. It was strength-sapping physical labor ten hours a day, helping to handle inch-thick bars of steel that were heated white-hot in a furnace and then pushed repeatedly through giant revolving cylinders until the metal had been thinned to layers of desired thickness. The heat was so intense, fifteen minutes at a time was all any man could endure before taking a break to cool off, and if he stood too long in one spot, the rubber soles of his boots melted. Hour after hour he trudged back to the rollers, so exhausted at night he could hardly walk home.

He finished out the summer, an experience he never forgot, but when vacation was over he went back to school with eager relief, glad to be a boy again and less anxious to hurry into giving it up. His marks remained excellent, and he was acknowledged as the school's best debater and began to lead other class activities. In the afternoons, he took to spending more time in the family's law office, and friends sometimes found him there reading his father's law books just for fun, fascinated by accounts of trials and cases, by the legal drama of courtroom testimony. He talked them over with his father, discussed the strategy of current cases, the conflicts involved and the important decisions that were won or lost on the basis of the sort of logical arguments he had enjoyed all his life.

Herman Willkie by then was rated by fellow attorneys as

among Indiana's best trial lawyers, although some of Elwood's more conservative citizens angrily denounced him as a radical, a Socialist or worse, because he represented the struggling new union trying to win recognition at the tinplate factory. In those days before adequate workmen's compensation laws, he also battled in court to collect medical payments for men injured at work, was the outspoken defender of workers in scores of other suits against big corporations and industries, a crusader against saloons, gambling joints, and political corruption that the "nice people" of Elwood preferred not to have exposed to public view. But Wendell took new pride in his father's work and in his mother's readiness to fight the legal battles at his side. His older brother Bob already had decided to study law, and he began to think of the profession as the one he wanted, too, but he knew it would mean years of study before he could be on his own. There was another call to adventure that tempted him.

Paul Harmon had quit school temporarily and headed West to try to make his fortune in Aberdeen, South Dakota, where the government was opening up free land to homesteaders. Paul had gotten a job as a cashier in a restaurant, and he wrote back that there was sure to be work for Wendell. The land rush had touched off a boom.

Wendell's father agreed to let him go during the summer vacation of 1909 so he could learn for himself what the West had to offer. He had some money saved from his work of the summer before at the tinplate mill, and his father bought him a one-way ticket to Aberdeen and told him that after that he would be strictly on his own. Gwyneth walked to the station with him to see him off.

Trains had progressed far beyond the iron horses that first carried travelers into the pioneer West, but it wasn't hard for Wendell to imagine that he was being drawn by a great iron

29

steed that belched smoke and cinders as the cars rattled across the endless expanse of farms and open land. In Aberdeen itself he found the West as wild as in any of the tales he had read about its earlier days. As Paul had written, the town was booming, overcrowded with men seeking new land and new lives. With the homesteaders had come a riff-raff of gamblers, drifters, and camp followers. Wendell had grown up in Elwood when it was a boom town, but it was never as rough and raw as this place that seemed to be bursting with challenges a seventeen-year-old was eager to meet.

Paul Harmon was waiting for him when he arrived and took him along the unpaved street to the square-fronted restaurant where they were to share a room. But his first job there was something of a letdown. The proprietor put him to work washing dishes in a kitchen foggy with the smoke of frying fat, and so steaming hot it reminded him of the furnace room at the tinplate mill. Meals were served continuously, and the flow of dirty dishes never seemed to stop.

After a week of it Wendell was given a chance to run the "hotel" the restaurant owner had established by putting up an old circus tent behind the restaurant and filling it with makeshift wooden bunks that were crowded together under the sagging canvas roof. Wendell was to get twenty cents of each half-dollar he could collect from anybody he might persuade to spend the night there, and much to the owner's surprise he filled the place almost every night. He did it by searching the town's streets for drunks, convincing them that it would be better to sleep in the "hotel" than in the gutter, and leading them back by the arm. Some he had to half-carry up an outside stairway at the side of the building and then down another flight to the tent at the rear because their condition was too disreputable for them to be taken through the restaurant.

When he had earned three hundred dollars, he decided it

was time to move on to something else. He wanted to go into business for himself but he meant to hoard his capital until he found some really promising enterprise. With a supply of sandwiches and a blanket, he hopped a freight train and began a boxcar journey farther west. Riding the rails, he made his way into Montana and Wyoming, picking up odd jobs now and then until he came to another boom town where opportunity seemed to await him in the form of a small plant for the making of cement blocks.

It was a bustling little community with new homes and buildings going up at a rapid rate, and after a quick survey and a hard sales talk by the promoter who owned the business, Wendell invested his money in the cement block machinery. It was only after the man quickly cleared out of town that he discovered it was impossible to freight in a supply of cement to make the blocks at any price that would allow for a profit. He went flat broke, was forced to abandon the business, and with less than five dollars in his pocket took to riding the rails again.

For a time he worked as a ranch hand, and then helped cut hay on a farm. He enjoyed it there until the farm family began to treat him as a son and tried to encourage him rather pointedly to take an interest in their daughter. When the farmer's wife began dropping broad hints that it might be a good place for him to settle down, Wendell rolled his few belongings into his blanket, walked into town, and boarded the next empty boxcar out.

He had heard from another rail-rider that Yellowstone National Park was hiring young men to drive groups of tourists around in sight-seeing coaches, so he hopped another freight car in that direction. He managed to convince Park officials he was an experienced driver although his only experience had been driving a one-horse bakery wagon over the flat country roads around Elwood. Given a stagecoach

31

and six-horse team to handle, only luck kept him from a serious accident on his first trip when the horses ran out of control down a rocky slope. His badly-shaken and frightened passengers complained and saw to it that he was promptly fired.

By then the summer was almost over and he decided to quit the West while he still had a little money saved from his work as a field hand. Weary of bumming his way by boxcar, he spent part of his money for a ticket to ride back home across the country to Elwood in a day coach, if not in style at least in comparative comfort. While he had been away the union had called a strike at the tinplate plant. The town was torn by a showdown labor battle, and Wendell's father, as the union's attorney, was in the thick of it.

Chapter Four

EMOTIONS had boiled over in strike-torn Elwood by the end of August, 1909, and Wendell became not only his father's office assistant but also his bodyguard to protect him from threatened violence. The strike was part of a walk-out by union metal workers at fifteen Midwestern plants of the corporation that had taken over the town's tinplate factory. Workers had struck in protest against new machine methods of production and the hiring of non-union labor, and the company had resolved to break the union, which it accused of trying to halt "industrial progress."

Wendell's father had advised the union against the strike because he felt it was still too weak in membership and lacked funds, but once it was called, he led the legal battle for the workers in the courts. Sitting in with his father at union strategy meetings, at court hearings and at conferences that attempted to bring some compromise with management, Wendell had a first-hand education in labor disputes. Visiting the homes of workers, he also saw their growing misery as the trouble dragged on, day after day, and men with no income, debts mounting, and credit cut off, struggled to provide food and necessities for their families.

Tempers flared when the company ran special trains of strike-breakers through the picket lines under armed protection. Women joined their men in the demonstrations against the strike-breakers, and one band of women hurled buckets of slops over "scabs" who tried to pass through the plant gates. Wendell's father went to court to defend those arrested and also fought long and finally successful court actions to block company attempts to obtain a Federal injunction against the picketing.

But the sympathy of the town, mainly with the strikers in the beginning, began to turn against them when the company threatened to shut down the plant permanently and deprive Elwood of its main industry. Some citizens demanded that the police "get tough" with the strikers, and there were fist-fights and minor brawls. Four strike-breakers imported from West Virginia were convicted of carrying concealed weapons, and charges were made that the company supplied others with arms. Wendell had to use his own fists once to defend his father when a bunch of toughs, inspired by too many drinks at a bar near the factory, cornered them one night and tried to push his father around, but the scuffle was a brief one and nobody was injured.

Fortunately, the tension that hung over Elwood failed to explode in any mass outburst, but the company did break the union temporarily. Dispirited and with their families going hungry, unable to hold out any longer, small groups of workers and then increasing numbers gave up the struggle and drifted back to the factory to seek their jobs again on the company's terms. The company resumed production and the strike eventually collapsed. But while the injunction action was pending in the courts the union considered seeking the help of famed liberal lawyer Clarence Darrow, and

34

Wendell accompanied his father and a union delegation to discuss it with Darrow in his Chicago office.

The union men found that Darrow's fee was more than they could afford, but for Wendell the visit was memorable not only because his father introduced him to Darrow as "my son and confidential assistant" but because the celebrated lawyer half-jokingly offered some practical advice when he learned that Wendell himself was thinking of a law career. Darrow had said his fee for taking the union case would be $20,000, plus a thousand dollars a day for his time in court, and he smiled and told Wendell, "It's a good thing for you to learn, son, that there is nothing unethical in being adequately compensated for advocating a cause in which you deeply believe."

Wendell still had to attend Elwood High School that fall to gain final credits in several subjects, but his average grades were so high he was excused from the last month of classes so he wouldn't have to wait another term to enter the University of Indiana at Bloomington. He went from high school to college without any time off in between. By the time he was officially listed among Elwood High School graduates at the end of January, 1910, he had been enrolled for about three weeks in the freshman class at the university. He was just about to celebrate his eighteenth birthday.

His brothers and sister Julia were already so well established on the campus that the university newspaper, the *Daily Student*, hailed the appearance of "the latest of the tribe of Willkie" with the headline: *Another Willkie Arrives*. Fred was one year ahead of Wendell, Julia was doing university graduate work and teaching classes at nearby Bloomington High School, and brother Bob also was teaching high school while waiting to complete his university law course.

Wendell joined the others in a small furnished cottage just off the campus that they had rented together to save money.

35

Julia acted as housekeeper for the lot of them, and living arrangements were free and easy, with even fewer restrictions than there had been at home. The Willkie campus dwelling was a social center for friends who came and went as they pleased, sprawled over the sofa and chairs, shared pick-up meals eaten when anybody was hungry enough to open a can of soup, and joined in penny-ante poker games or in the arguments that could be expected whenever there was one or more Willkie present.

Although Wendell thought the peaked green cap all freshmen were required to wear made him look silly, he donned it with only mild protest and immediately tried to join in every available activity. He impressed a freshman classmate as a lanky giant, rushing back and forth across the hilly snow-covered paths among the big brick and limestone buildings of the wooded campus as though he meant to take the university's citadel of knowledge by storm. Surprisingly, though, some of his first instructors found him rather shy and for all the reputation his sister and brothers had gained before him, he personally created little stir on the campus during his first term.

He stayed on for the university's summer session to crowd in as much extra classwork as he could, but he did manage to get home to Elwood for a few weeks with his family, to bolster his college funds by clerking part time in a fruit store, and to share some summer evenings with Gwyneth, who had graduated from Elwood High School in June. On his way back to his own classes at Bloomington that fall, he took Gwyneth to Indianapolis so she could enroll at Butler University, and soon was visiting her every chance he got, bringing roses when he could afford them or boxes of candy bars he knew she liked.

Paul Harmon, who had given up his Western adventures soon after Wendell had, joined him at the university, and

George De Hority was among other old friends from Elwood who were there. Many of his campus friends, old and new, had become fraternity members but Wendell refused several bids and took a firm stand against all Greek letter societies. His strong feeling against them came in part from Woodrow Wilson, the political idol of his college years and a lasting influence upon the shaping of his own political philosophy. Wilson, then governor of New Jersey, had first come into national prominence as president of Princeton University where his democratic reforms had included an unsuccessful attempt to put an end to the exclusive upper-class eating clubs which were Princeton's equivalent of fraternities. Much publicity had been given to Wilson's quarrel with Princeton's trustees over the campus organizations. Wilson argued that the clubs interfered with studies and became so important in students' lives that they distracted them from the real purpose of education, that they frequently had a cruel and lasting effect upon those whose lack of wealth or family background kept them from membership, and that they exercised control by the privileged few over all campus activities and were basically undemocratic.

Wendell, facing the fraternity question himself at the start of his university life, thoroughly agreed with Wilson's views and decided that the battle should be fought at Indiana as it had been at Princeton. He started arguing against fraternities with everybody he met, soon found himself spokesman for a non-fraternity group of students who felt as he did, and became the campus leader of the "barbarians."

It was no small shock to him when he learned that Gwyneth, in defiance of his views, had joined a sorority. Wanting to enjoy the fun and social good times of college life at Butler, she had accepted a bid from Kappa Alpha Theta. They argued, but she had made up her mind. She told him that fraternity life would be good for him, too, that

37

it would help give him the "polish" he lacked. His visits tu see her at Butler became somewhat awkward since fraternities and sororities monopolized the social life there as well as at Indiana University, and he was an outsider to her group. But they still dated, and when he went off to Northern Indiana the next summer with his brother Bob to take a vacation job on a farm he walked four miles a day into town and back to mail his letters to Gwyneth.

When he wasn't working in the fields that summer of 1911, Wendell spent most of his time reading the books he had brought along. Among them was *Das Kapital* by Karl Marx, which aroused his curiosity to know more about Socialism and led him to read the works of Herbert Spencer and Edward Bellamy. When he returned to the university at the end of summer, he suggested to his economics professor that there should be a course in Socialism so that people who were always talking about it would at least know what they were talking about. The professor agreed and said that if Wendell could round up ten or twelve students who were interested he would offer a formal class. Wendell drummed up a class, but also started talk around the campus that he was a wild-eyed radical.

"I had to buttonhole almost everyone in the university before I could get the ten," he said later. "It's no wonder I got a reputation as a Socialist." Another time, years afterwards, he also said: "Any man who is not something of a Socialist before he is forty has no heart; any man who is still a Socialist after he is forty has no head."

When he helped organize a Friday evening group to discuss social problems, with various professors as speakers, the university yearbook, the *Arbutus,* dubbed it *The Socialist Club.* But it was his stand against the fraternity system, not his youthful curiosity about Socialism, that led to his first direct venture into campus politics. Deciding to challenge the domination of the fraternities, he persuaded Paul Harmon to run as a non-fraternity candidate for president of the sophomore class. Paul treated it as a joke, thinking he had no chance. But as his manager, Wendell unified the barbs, took advantage of a quarrel among the fraternities over which of several candidates to back, and waged a campaign that won Paul the election.

The success made Wendell a recognized power in campus politics and encouraged him to campaign for reforms in the Student Union and other groups. There were few protest meetings of any kind in which he didn't have a voice, or demonstrations in which he didn't join, and as one friend put it: "Wen marched in every shirt-tail parade he didn't lead."

He and his friends helped revive the university's Jackson Democratic Club, and as the national elections of 1912 approached, he became an ardent leader of the campus supporters of Woodrow Wilson. In Jackson Club debates he was willing to concede there might be some Republicans who were not all bad, especially among the progressives who were trying to reform the party and wrest control of it from the conservative Old Guard. But as a Democrat from childhood, his wish for most Republicans was that they would be thoroughly defeated. In Wilson he had found a man who eloquently voiced his own beliefs and whose call for a "New Freedom" became a lasting statement of Wendell Willkie's faith in middle-of-the-road democracy.

America had to free itself from the domination of the trusts and the privileged men of money and power, Wilson declared, so that business could flourish in open competition that would preserve free enterprise, and so the government would be cleansed of boss control and corruption, and return its decisions to the people. "We have been proud of our industrial achievements," Wilson said, "but we have not hitherto stopped thoughtfully enough to count the human cost.

39

Our duty is to cleanse, to reconsider, to restore . . . every process of our common life."

At a mock Democratic National Convention staged by the Jackson Club, Wendell took a stand in support of Wilsonian principles that would be echoed in his own political speeches for the next thirty years. And in November 1912, when Wilson was swept into the White House by an overwhelming victory which carried forty states, Wendell also won an election on the campus to the Jackson Club's executive board.

Other honors came his way. He was on the executive committee of the Student Council and the Interclass Athletic Committee. As a member and then president of the Indiana University Boosters Club he promoted an interscholastic basketball tournament in which ninety-five teams from all over the state took part, organized it, worked out the schedules, secured the referees, directed the printing of tickets and programs, and made all arrangements to house and feed the teams.

He was chosen a Student Marshal from among those whose qualifications were listed as being "representative students, popular among the student body, possessing influential ability, and whose scholarship is above question," a group selected by the faculty from candidates nominated by student organizations to preserve orderly conduct at athletic contests and other gatherings. Surprisingly, for one who had been so opposed to campus conformity, he also became head of the Board of Traditions, charged with seeing to it that all freshmen wore their green caps and otherwise obeyed the rules of upperclassmen.

His free and easy cottage life ended when Julia and his brothers finished their university work and went on to other things, Julia to teach languages at a school in North Manchester, Bob to pursue his law career, and Fred to Puerto

Rico as a chemist for a sugar company. With the breaking up of the "Willkie tribe," Wendell became a dormitory resident and seemed content to settle down as a generally well-liked and respected campus citizen.

Although he still enjoyed arguing with his professors, especially those he admired most, philosophy professor Ernest Lindley and history professor James Woodburn, he was less rebellious than in his first university years. Always a heavy reader, he began to spend even more time in the library, and in long contemplative walks about the campus. Doctor W. A. Jenkins, the university librarian, told a group discussing the merits of various students that Wendell was "more widely read than any other boy I have ever known."

He took to the platform at campus rallies to tell applauding fellow students, "I am an unorganized man and I am proud of it," and he continued his campaign against the fraternities, but in private conversations he sometimes grudgingly admitted to friends that the fraternity system was not the total evil he had once thought it to be. His best friends in his senior year, those with whom he associated in leading campus activities, were mostly fraternity men, and they became convinced that his views had somewhat mellowed.

George De Hority and several others decided to make a determined effort to bring him into their fraternity, Beta Theta Pi. The brothers formally extended an invitation, and George and the others did all they could to pressure him into accepting, arguing that it would be for his own good in future years. When he still refused, George went to Indianapolis and asked Gwyneth to use her influence to make Wendell accept. Gwyneth believed as his friends did that he was passing up a fellowship that could only be to his own benefit and that he would regret it after he left the university. The issue had been a constant one between them, and she had run out of arguments, so she agreed the time had come to

41

settle it. Gwyneth told Wendell he had to become a member or give her up.

He begged her to change her mind, made a trip to Indianapolis to enlist the support of some of her own friends but they sided with Gwyneth and she was adamant. In later years, he was able to smile over the melodramatic way he had reacted to Gwyneth's ultimatum, but to a young man in love, torn by the intense conflict of loyalties, the decision he faced was a tragic one. His roommate, Maurice Bluhm, found him distraught and disheveled, pacing the room. "If I don't join, I'll lose my girl," he told Maurice, "but if I do, I'll lose my soul."

After nights of lost sleep and days of troubled indecision, he joined Beta Theta Pi. But he refused to be initiated until the last day of his final term, when the non-fraternity men he had championed would be leaving the university with him and there would be no way his fraternity membership could be used to influence campus politics. As a symbol of her victory, he sent Gwyneth the fraternity pin he had never wanted.

Yet, with all his personal torment, his world was still a tranquil one when he graduated in June, 1913, a man of twenty-one in a complacent and prosperous land whose people felt protected and far removed from the troubles of Europe, enjoying its last year of peace. He had won academic honors, with most of his credit hours in A and B grades, and had crowded so much extra pre-law study into his undergraduate years that he needed only one more year of credits to earn his law degree.

He had long since decided that law would be his career, but before he could go on to complete law school, he had to earn the money to finance it. The Willkies still had a younger brother and sister to put through college, and now that he was a man he felt he should no longer rely on family funds for his own advanced study, so as a temporary second choice he meant to follow his father's example and start as a teacher. With the help of Professor Woodburn, who recommended him, Wendell Willkie went to Coffeyville, Kansas, to earn the money he wanted for law school as a high school teacher of history.

Chapter Five

COFFEYVILLE, Kansas, had outgrown its wild days as a frontier town where the long cattle trails from Texas met the railroad and had become a farming community by the time Lewis W. Willkie, as the high school's new history teacher identified himself, arrived in September, 1913. But the great 1889 land rush, from there across the border into Oklahoma, was still part of the town's living memory, the notorious Dalton gang had been shot down in Coffeyville during an attempted bank robbery only twenty years in the past, and the dust of adventure had hardly settled upon the boom days of discovery in nearby oil fields.

For him, it offered "my first real adventure in standing on my own feet," as he later put it, and was "the happiest time I ever had." He "reveled completely in new contacts and experiences" and did not have "a single sour memory of the year I spent in Coffeyville." It was a place he remembered fondly all his life. In Coffeyville, he said, "I learned much more than I taught."

As a teacher, he brought Coffeyville some of the same young enthusiasm Philip Bing had given Elwood High. He

44

was careful to dress correctly in a conservative dark suit and to wear a stiff-collared white shirt, but there was no formality in his classes. Acting out some historic scene, he would pace the room, wave his arms, pound the desk. He encouraged argument and debate, and made the events of history vivid by dramatizing them and relating them to his students' lives. If he could make a point by telling a joke, he would, and if he thought the class had earned a recess he might order history books put away while he sat on the corner of his desk and read aloud a short story from O. Henry.

Like Bing, he was idolized by some of the boys in his classes and adored by the girls, and school board member Charles Carpenter described him as "a radiant and eager young man who won enthusiastic devotion." He started a literary society, a debating team that successfully challenged other schools for miles around, coached a track team that won all its events, set up a basketball team for girls, and led a boys' basketball team to victory in six of ten scheduled games. He was chief cheerleader at pep rallies, and when there were celebration bonfires, he shucked his coat and collar and helped the boys stack crates for burning.

Coffeyville opened its doors to him with warm hospitality and with invitations to dinner, to parties, and even to go on a star-gazing expedition in the interests of amateur astronomy. Caught up in a busy new life, his days filled with teaching and his nights with the fun of being an admired young man about town, his letters to Gwyneth became less frequent. He did see her during his vacation, home in Indiana the next summer, but the relationship that had been part of their years of growing up somehow had changed, as the whole world around him seemed to be changing. In August, to the shock of most Americans who had paid little attention to the long-smoldering rivalries in Europe, the German army invaded Belgium. The war "over there" still seemed far away,

45

but the news of it filled him with a restlessness about the world's uncertain future and his own, a desire to escape his too-familiar surroundings, to seek adventure again, freedom, and challenge.

He had hardly returned to Coffeyville from his vacation when his brother Fred, who had gone to Puerto Rico as a chemist for the Fajardo Sugar Company, wrote to offer him a job there in the testing laboratory. The pay was more than the eighty-five dollars a month he got for teaching history, and it would get him to law school sooner and also give him a chance to see a little more of the world. His students were unhappy when he announced that he was leaving in November 1914. They arranged a special testimonial program "for one of the best friends C.H.S. has ever known" and the whole student body and most of the town went to the station to see him off. His cheering admirers all but mobbed him with hugs and handshakes, and one girl rushed forward to kiss him as he stepped aboard the train.

Arriving back in Elwood in time for Paul Harmon's wedding to Rose Dickerson, he and his old friend got into a debate that became a legend. Nobody remembered afterwards what started the marathon discussion, but they argued through most of the night before the ceremony, picked it up again in the morning, went on debating while Paul hurriedly dressed, and paused only during the wedding itself before resuming their verbal contest at the reception. When the bride, understandably impatient by then, told the groom to break it off or they would miss the train for their wedding trip, Willkie said he would go along with them part of the way so he and Paul could "finish this." To the amazement of their friends, who ever afterwards delighted in repeating the story, he boarded the train and went on arguing until Paul, under his bride's icy stare, finally conceded defeat and Will-

46

kie departed at the next station to let the couple continue their honeymoon alone.

There was a delay in final arrangements for the job in Puerto Rico, so Willkie decided to take a brief refresher course in chemistry at Oberlin College in Ohio, where his younger brother Ed could be his roommate. Ed, however, soon got an appointment to the Naval Academy at Annapolis where he was to become an outstanding Olympic athlete, an intercollegiate track and wrestling champion, and All-American star tackle of Navy's football team.

Gwyneth was planning to teach school in Elwood after finishing at Butler, and Willkie's plans to go to Puerto Rico brought them to the realization that they had been gradually drifting apart and the time had come to break the ties. They both felt, as Gwyneth later said, "that it had gone on too long." After awhile she married someone else, and years afterwards when Willkie's presidential candidacy brought to light the story of the girl he had first loved, he wrote to apologize for all the unwanted publicity given their youthful romance, and they exchanged a few friendly and chatty letters about their respective families.

After six weeks of cramming chemistry at Oberlin, Willkie sailed to Puerto Rico to start his new job with the Fajardo Sugar Company in January 1915, and discovered that very little knowledge of chemistry was required. For twelve hours a day he had to take sample after sample during the refining process and make simple control tests, most of which showed hardly any variation. Sweating in the heat and bored by the monotonous routine, he still had to be constantly alert to guard against any fractional change that might ruin thousands of dollars worth of sugar. His boss praised him for the responsible way he did the job, but Willkie said it was a good thing no skill was needed because he

47

broke more test tubes than anybody else who had ever worked there.

The sugar company dominated the small seaport town of Fajardo and everything else in the area, but he made friends among the Puerto Ricans and enjoyed whatever recreation was available in the evenings. He liked to wander down to the plaza where men gathered on the benches to talk or play cards in the twilight, and on his days off he traveled the whole island to visit historic forts and churches, climb the mountains and walk the beaches and fields of sugar cane.

He wanted to learn more about the people and how they lived, but what he learned disturbed him. In this beautiful island paradise of strange bright flowers, green hills, and lush tropical growth, there was illiteracy, disease, and squalor such as he had never imagined. Large families of workers were crowded into one-room earth-floored shacks. Mercilessly exploited, those who were able to get work were paid only thirty cents a day, and then only during the six months a year they were needed in the fields.

While he was there some of the workers broke into rebellion. Willkie happened to be riding horseback through the fields one day with one of the bosses, having a casual conversation with the man, when a half-starved rebel stumbled out of the sugar cane where he had been hiding. The manager hacked at the worker with his cane knife, all but cutting off his shoulder as he felled him, and went right on with the ride and the conversation. The awful memory was still in Willkie's mind twenty-five years later. When a magazine editor asked him why, as a wealthy man, he didn't think like a typical American millionaire, Willkie told him the story of that horseback ride in the sugar fields of Puerto Rico and said, "If there was any single incident, it was that."

He had earned the money to see him through his last year of study by the time the slack season came to Puerto Rico, and six months there had been enough. He returned to El-wood in July, 1915, and that fall went back to the University of Indiana, a serious-minded young man of twenty-three, determined to make the most of the year's work that would bring him his law degree.

Willkie welcomed his once reluctant membership in Beta Theta Pi for the new friends it brought him since most of his old friends had left the university in the two years he had been away, and he roomed near the fraternity house and spent much of his free time there. In school elections that fall he was chosen class orator. He also led a delegation that appeared at a meeting of the Bloomington City Council to argue unsuccessfully that students of legal age should be granted the vote in Bloomington elections because being at college deprived them of their chance to vote at home. But his main interest, aside from his studies, was in debating the issue that had emotionally divided the nation, the great question of American neutrality in the war that ravaged Europe.

German torpedoes had sunk the liner *Lusitania* off the coast of Ireland the summer before, and continuing U-boat attacks had taken two hundred American lives as Germany tried to break England's blockade of the seas. Submarines were striking without warning at merchant vessels carrying supplies to the Allies who had placed enormous orders for food and munitions in the United States, and Germany was being denounced as an autocratic nation ready to impose its military might upon the world.

With his long family tradition of hatred against German militarism, Willkie found his faith in Woodrow Wilson somewhat shaken by the President's reluctance to abandon the policy of neutrality. As an about-to-be lawyer, he argued that Germany clearly was the violator of international law. He approved Wilson's attempts to restore peace, if there was

49

any chance of that, and didn't believe in war as a way of settling disputes among nations, but he did believe that America couldn't turn its back on what soon would be called a "struggle to make the world safe for democracy."

Yet for all his outspoken concern over world problems and his seriousness in applying himself to his law studies, his university year wasn't entirely a grind of books and debates. With Gwyneth in the past, he was free to date other girls and enjoy a full social life. An easy mixer and good talker, he was a popular guest at parties, and the frequent dinner or theater companion of several young ladies whose families he visited in Indianapolis. But none of them attracted him as much as a girl he met in the nearby farming community of Rushville.

His old friend George De Hority was marrying Louise Mauzy of Rushville and had asked him to be an usher at the wedding there. At a party for the couple the night before the ceremony, Willkie was introduced to one of Louise's bridesmaids, Edith Wilk. She was a vivacious blue-eyed girl with chestnut hair, and he joked about the similarity of their names. "Wilk and Willkie should go well together," he said. "We'll make good partners for George's wedding."

He soon learned that her father's people, like his, had come from Germany and that her mother's Scotch-Irish ancestors had come to America before the Revolution. Although she had been born in Nashville, Tennessee, her family had moved to Rushville when she was seven, and she considered it her real home. Her father was a building contractor who had built the Rush County courthouse, and she was the town's assistant librarian. She had gone to Indiana University for a year, but had left just before he began his first term. They talked of the campus, of books and libraries, and of his coming career as a lawyer. During the rest of the wedding festivities, they paired off together, and before he left to go back to his classes at Bloomington he knew that her nickname was "Billie" and that he wanted to see her again.

Although she seemed to enjoy his company as their friendship grew, some of her friends were less enthusiastic about him. Edith Wilk was a popular girl, with a string of would-be suitors, and they felt he was far from being the handsomest young man she knew or socially the most polished. One of her friends, who was critical of the talkative law student in whom she seemed to be taking such an interest, admitted that he might be smart when it came to books but that he didn't even know how to dance.

That winter, Willkie's faith in Woodrow Wilson was fully restored when the President finally announced a program of preparedness, and toured the country to arouse America to the view that the best way to "keep out of war" was to make the nation so strong nobody would dare attack. Monster preparedness parades were held in cities across the land, and Wilson himself marched in the one in Washington, even while he continued his diplomatic efforts to bring a negotiated peace in Europe.

Willkie took the lead in trying to organize another mock Democratic National Convention to be held by the university's Jackson Club on a Saturday afternoon. He set the date, and the *Daily Student* carried a notice that "Chairman Lewis W. Willkie is very anxious that anyone who can make a speech, fill an office, control a delegation, or participate in the affair at all" should get in touch with the committee. But in his preoccupation with politics, Willkie had forgotten that Indiana's annual baseball game with Purdue was scheduled for the same Saturday. When the day came, almost the whole student body went off to the ball game, and the Jackson Club had to cancel the mock convention.

As a member of the university debating team, he helped

win nine out of sixteen debates against other colleges, and his solid studying during the year brought him the honor of being named the "best all-around student" among law school seniors, which gained him the prize of a forty-three volume law encyclopedia. He was chosen to deliver the law school graduation address at an assembly which would include not only students and the entire faculty but also some of the state's prominent jurists and leaders of the Indiana bar.

Willkie decided he would give no ordinary speech filled with expected platitudes. He meant to challenge his listeners, shake their conventional attitudes, awaken them to the liberal reforms he fervently believed were needed in government and industry. Friends who read the rough draft of his speech warned him it would create an uproar, but that was what he hoped it would do. He deliberately set out to shock his complacent audience into considering ideas they too seldom thought about.

Borrowing the title from Woodrow Wilson, he called his address *The New Freedom*. There is no known text of what he said, but published reports of the affair agree that he boldly attacked the conservatism of his own law school as well as the members of the state supreme court. He waded two-fistedly into the touchiest issue then before Indiana's voters and called for a new state constitution so Indiana could follow Wilson's lead and enact state laws to regulate business and banking for the common good.

Highly dramatized versions of what happened that graduation day have pictured the eminent jurists and distinguished lawyers as sputtering in red-faced rage when Willkie perspiringly finished his speech and was led by the arm from the platform by the embarrassed law school dean while the audience sat in shocked and stony silence. Perhaps the reports were exaggerated, but his speech undoubtedly caused a sensation. Nearly twenty-five years later, a faculty

52

member still recalled it as "the most radical speech you ever heard." Willkie was severely reprimanded, and there was some talk that he might be refused his diploma and his graduation might be delayed. But he received his law degree, was admitted to the bar, and, if nothing else, certainly had brought himself to the attention of Indiana's legal fraternity.

When he went home to Elwood in June 1916, he decided to test his mettle before he joined his father and brother Bob in the family law firm by getting himself deputized as a temporary county attorney so he could oppose his father in his first court case. It involved a man accused of burning down a neighbor's barn in a fit of anger. There were no witnesses and little actual evidence so Willkie, as acting prosecutor, decided to sway the jury by delivering a long talk about the history of the crime of arson and the reasons for the stiff laws against it. When he finally finished what turned into an hour-long harangue, his father approached the jury as the defender of the accused man. He smiled and said, "I believe my son will make a great lawyer some day. He can make so very much out of so very little." The jurors roared with laughter and promptly returned a verdict of "not guilty," and Willkie ruefully admitted that with all he had learned at the university his father could still teach him a few things about handling a jury.

While most of the cases he argued for his father's firm were minor ones, they gave him solid grounding in the trial and error of courtroom tactics, and although much of his work was in the office, helping to prepare cases and handling legal routine, his father saw to it that he gained as much experience as possible in lower courts around the county. Some of his suits were for damage claims involving the automobiles that finally were coming into widespread use.

Willkie made several attempts to drive a car himself but

admitted that he probably was the poorest driver in the county. Never much interested in anything mechanical, he was likely to get warmed up to an argument and forget that he had to hold the steering wheel. Once, when his brother Ed was riding with him, they got into an argument and the next thing he knew, the car was off the road and turned over in a ditch. Willkie crawled out but Ed was pinned under the car. Frightened, he dropped to his knees and clawed at the dirt with his hands to uncover his brother's face. Ed was rescued, but Willkie was so shaken he never liked to drive after that. Later on, he did buy a car of his own, but he sold it after a few months and never bought another. All the rest of his life he avoided driving an automobile, although he enjoyed traveling by car as long as someone else was at the wheel and he wasn't forced to keep his attention on the road.

As usual, he enjoyed provoking arguments wherever he went, and the law office became something of an informal debating society. He had joined the Elks, and, as an officer of the Elwood lodge, ceremoniously opened and closed the meetings with dramatic ritual. But for the most part he was reluctant to join clubs, shunned group conformity, and took little interest in community affairs. He had made up his mind that he didn't intend to settle down in Elwood and make a career of becoming a small-town lawyer, and was hopeful that through political connections he could get some sort of a legal position with the state.

Rushville was too far away for the convenient pursuit of courtship, and so was Edith Wilk, and to improve that situation he enlisted the help of his friend George De Hority. George's wife Louise wrote to urge Edith to come and join her in Elwood so they could renew the companionship they had enjoyed in Rushville before Louise married. She told Edith that there "just happened" to be an opening for a li-

54

brarian at the Elwood library, a position that paid sixty-five dollars a month and was well suited to Edith's library experience. Perhaps it didn't "just happen" that Edith was offered the job, since Willkie's parents had founded the library, and he was about to become a member of the board. On September 5, 1916, the minutes of the Elwood library board meeting included the notation that "a Miss Wilk of Rushville will accept the position of librarian here."

Willkie arranged for her to room with his aunt, and prepared to sweep her off her feet from the moment she arrived, but Edith Wilk was not about to be convinced that easily. A level-headed young woman who meant to take her own time to make up her mind, she showed her independence by dating other young men to whom she was introduced in Elwood, and when Willkie tried to be with her alone, he usually found himself part of a congenial foursome that included George and Louise.

By then he had firmly made up his own mind that he wanted her as his wife, but when his proposals became too ardent, she decided to go back to Rushville to think things over in the calmer surroundings of her own home. In mid-November she asked the library board to choose a successor as soon as possible so that she could leave. She returned to Rushville, but Willkie didn't give her much chance to think things out alone. In actual straightline distance, Rushville was about sixty-five miles from Elwood, but to get there he had to make a roundabout interurban trip through Indianapolis that meant up to five hours of traveling back and forth. That didn't stop him. He became practically a commuter, bringing her candy and flowers, and trying to win the support of her mother and father and all her friends.

Some thought they were an oddly-matched couple, Willkie so towering big and bold, and Edith so small and dainty, but those who spoke of the attraction of opposites possibly

55

judged by outward appearance. Mary Sleeth, Rushville's chief librarian and Edith's close friend, who years later became manager of Willkie's Indiana farms, thought Edith must have been attracted by "his brains, not his looks" because he "wasn't any fashion-plate type."

As love led Willkie to Rushville that winter, lost in his own romantic world, President Wilson made his last attempts to mediate the war. He tried to get the warring powers to state their terms for peace and in a speech before the Senate in January, he first proposed what someday was to become the League of Nations. Wilson declared that the war must be followed "by some definite concert of power which will make it virtually impossible that any such catastrophe should ever overwhelm us again" and that the American people must be willing to give "formal and solemn adherence" to some kind of international peace-keeping organization or "League for Peace."

Wilson's proposal seemed to Willkie then, and increasingly in the years to come, the best hope of mankind. But talk of future peace became futile as the war raged on, and all negotiations failed. Germany again embarked upon unrestricted submarine warfare, and the United States broke diplomatic relations with Germany. In April, the fateful decision came, and the United States declared itself forced to join in the war that was "to end wars," to preserve the rights of democracy that were "more precious than peace."

In Rushville, Willkie finally had won Edith Wilk's consent. They were engaged and would be married. But now there were all the immediate uncertainties of war, and their personal plans had to wait.

Chapter Six

THE *Elwood Call-Leader* reported on May 11, 1917, that Lewis Wendell Willkie was among those who had departed for active service in the first Officers' Training group established at Fort Benjamin Harrison, near Indianapolis. An Army clerk, making out the official records, reversed his first and middle names, and Willkie never bothered after that to correct those who thought he had been named Wendell Lewis instead of Lewis Wendell.

His first days at training camp reminded him of those spent as a boy during the summer at Culver Military Academy, with the constant drills, regulations and uniformed regimentation he had so detested. During the twenty-two months he spent in the Army, his inner rebellion against military conformity never ceased but he managed to accommodate himself to the facts of Army life he couldn't change. His sense of rhythm was never keen, and learning to march in step with the others reminded him of the trouble he had had as a boy when he read poetry aloud and was likely to accent the wrong syllables. Another difficulty was his lack of any sense of time. When he was interested in something, time meant little to him and he found it hard to become used to the military day with activities regulated to specified hours. In later years, he never wore or carried a watch, refusing to be made conscious of the pressure of minutes by any ticking device on his person. He said that if it was ever really vital to know what time it was, he could always ask somebody.

But he did thoroughly enjoy the comradeship of the Army, and he endured the monotony, accepted the regulations as much as he had to, and went on living very much his own life within the limitations enforced upon him. On August 15, 1915, he graduated among Fort Harrison's first crop of ninety-day officers and was commissioned a first lieutenant in the infantry. Along with Donald Thornburgh, a friend from Indiana University who was to become his close Army pal, he was assigned to the Infantry School of Arms at Harvard for a month's intensive training in basic infantry tactics under a staff of French officers who were battle combat veterans.

As a young lieutenant, Willkie had no part in the active campus life at Harvard, but his return to the halls of learning rekindled his interest in history, and he convinced his friend Thornburgh that instead of studying manuals of infantry tactics, they should spend their free time making historic pilgrimages. Together they journeyed from Cambridge to nearby Plymouth Rock, Bunker Hill, Lexington and Concord, and one weekend took the train as far as New Haven to see the statue of Nathan Hale. The jaunts established a pattern Willkie followed after that wherever he traveled. Sometimes, even if it meant going miles out of his way, he made it a point to visit the historic sites of an area, to walk over the ground and try to imagine himself part of the event that had made history so he could better understand the experience lived through by those who had been there years before.

When their month's training at Harvard was over, Willkie

and Thornburgh learned that, having drilled them in infantry tactics, the Army had decided to make artillery officers of them. Assigned to the 325th Field Artillery, they reluctantly boarded a train for Camp Zachary Taylor, near Louisville, Kentucky, where they strongly protested that they had been trained to command foot soldiers and knew nothing at all about firing big guns. But a tough old regular Army major took them aside to assure them that their lack of knowledge was shared by their fellow officers. "You don't have to worry because they don't know anything either," he said. "All they've learned is the names of things."

While Willkie's unit marked time in Kentucky for almost a year, he and Edith decided, whatever plans the Army might have for him, that they would go through with their own interrupted plans to marry. All arrangements were made to have the wedding on Saturday, January 12, in Rushville. Willkie asked Thornburgh to be his best man, and they were granted weekend leave to make the trip. But on Friday night, Louisville was struck by a record blizzard and by morning all roads out of camp were blocked. There was no transportation and not even Army trucks could move.

Willkie and Thornburgh set out on foot through drifts that in some places were hip deep. Before they reached the suburbs, their hands and legs were numb and Willkie's ears were nearly frozen. A woman who saw them stumbling along the street invited them into her house to get warm, and they learned from her that there was one interurban car line still running into Louisville. They made it into the city, and Willkie went to the florist shop where he had arranged to pick up a wedding bouquet of white orchids and lilies of the valley. After a long wait in the cold station, they boarded the train for Rushville, but it became stalled in the snow about twenty miles out.

They hiked from the train to a livery stable in a nearby

small town and tried to hire horses, but the stable owner refused because the snow was too deep even for horses. By then it was long past time for the wedding. Dejectedly, Willkie and Thornburgh went to the town's only hotel and he phoned from there almost every hour to try to reassure the bride he had left waiting at the church. When Sunday morning came, the tracks to Rushville were still blocked so they decided to board a train in the other direction to Indianapolis where Thornburgh's family lived. Thornburgh's mother did what she could to repair the wilted wedding bouquet while they desperately tried to arrange some roundabout transportation.

Their Army leave was running out, and they were due back in camp Monday morning, so after he phoned Edith again Willkie put in a call to the regimental commander to plead for more time. His leave was extended another day, but Thornburgh's wasn't, and Willkie had to go on to Rushville without his best man. At last, two days late, he reached his bride-to-be. Late on Monday, January 14, 1918, Edith Wilk became Mrs. Wendell Willkie. Dressed in white satin, she held the remains of the frozen bouquet her bridegroom had carried to her through the storm.

Tuesday morning he went back to Camp Taylor alone, but Edith joined him as soon as she could. She found a place to live, across the Ohio River from Louisville in New Albany, and they had two months together before the Army sent him to Oklahoma late in March for training at the Fort Sill artillery school. Since they had no idea how long he would be assigned there or where he would go next, Edith went back home to Rushville to stay with her family.

Part of the training at Fort Sill involved an observation balloon group, and Willkie got into an argument over whether it was really dangerous to jump out of a balloon by parachute. Someone dared him to try, and bet him fifty dollars he wouldn't have the nerve. Rather than lose the argument, he said that he would if the commanding officer gave permission. He expected he would be forbidden to jump without proper training, but the commander said he had some parachutes he had been wanting to test and that if Willkie wanted to risk his life on a dare it was all right with him.

They strapped a parachute on him, told him how to pull the rip cord, and bundled him into a balloon. The balloonist was a French officer and very casual about the whole thing. He chatted with his thoroughly frightened passenger until they got up about fifteen hundred feet and then looked at the instruments and said, "Well, if I were going to jump, I would do it now." As Willkie told the story: "There wasn't anything for me to do but go over the side of the basket, which I did, pulled the rip cord as I had been instructed, landed safely and collected fifty dollars." He admitted it had been a foolhardy thing to do, but added, "If you are going into a war you can't be a coward."

Willkie's superior officers at Fort Sill recognized his ability to get things done, but some of them were sorely troubled by his unmilitary appearance and his disregard for the code of the armed services that set officers apart from enlisted men. He never acquired the neatness or bearing of the traditional officer. His shoulders slumped, his stride was lumbering, and he was apt to unhook his collar, roll up his sleeves, prop his shoes on a desk, and slouch back in the easiest chair he could find. He liked to sit in the kitchen and chat with the mess sergeant, and preferred the relaxed companionship of the enlisted men in the barracks to the somewhat stuffy atmosphere of the officers' club. He never pulled rank and, in fact, when he came into a barracks unexpectedly and saw a group of men about to spring to attention, he would call out, "Relax, it's just me."

After ten weeks' training at Fort Sill, he returned to Camp Taylor to take command of Battery F of his regiment. Eight days later, the regiment was ordered to West Point, Kentucky, and finally in early September, to Camp Upton, Long Island, where much to Willkie's delight, his wife managed to join him briefly for a few days before he was shipped overseas. He sailed for Europe on the crowded British troopship *Canada* on September 9, 1918. The ship was separated from its destroyer escort during part of the voyage and was in danger of attack from German U-boats, but a fellow officer recalled that Willkie was so involved in debate over pre-Civil War history with a sergeant from Georgia that he seemed totally unconcerned about the threat of enemy submarines. He also was one of the few who wasn't seasick from the rough passage.

They arrived in Scotland, and while they were camped at Winchester, waiting to be moved on, Willkie again took up his hobby of visiting nearby historic places. When some of the men asked to join him, he and another officer organized regular sightseeing hikes that finally attracted a group of about two hundred soldiers, with Willkie giving them informal lectures on the history of ancient Scottish castles, and monuments erected to commemorate the battles of other wars.

He and his men were brought back to the hardships of their own war by being forced to march on foot twenty-five miles a day under full pack all the way to Southampton because a rail strike had halted trains. Exhausted, they boarded the ship that took them to France and when they landed at Le Havre had to make another long hike to camp. There the war was made starkly real for them by their first sight of wounded soldiers.

Dirty, weary, disheveled, still with hardly any rest, they

went by train to Bordeaux and then to Camp De Souge, where they arrived in a cold and drizzling rain to take up quarters established on the soggy terrain of what had once been a forest preserve of the old pre-Revolutionary kings of France. The rain kept up for days, and they wallowed through the mud while undergoing final training by French artillery officers.

Willkie was recommended for promotion to captain by his regimental commander and eagerly awaited the order that would give him his new rank. What came instead was an order to move up to the front. He and his men were packing their gear to board the waiting trains that would take them into battle when another announcement came. The Armistice had been signed and the war was over. But his own Army service wasn't to end for another three months, and although he was overjoyed by the news of the Armistice, he was bitterly disappointed to learn that all ranks had been frozen. Since the Army needed no more officers, promotions were suspended and he wasn't to become a captain after all.

Most of the books he had been reading in his spare time were on military law and he put his studies to use defending men who were court-martialed. Under the Army code, any accused soldier could ask any officer to defend him, and Willkie had handled some cases before the Armistice. With the fighting at an end, he gradually became the unofficial defense attorney for his whole regiment. In the idle hours of waiting to be shipped home, some soldiers without a war to fight naturally got into trouble and some officers, fearing a loss of discipline, court-martialed men for what Willkie considered minor violations such as failing to get back to camp on time, getting into a brawl, or taking pot shots at some farmer's cow.

Willkie, as usual, welcomed any chance to put up an argu-

63

ment, especially in the defense of enlisted men against stiff-necked rules and regulations. He thoroughly enjoyed confronting the accusing officers, and his enthusiasm on the side of the men, plus his knowledge of law, won so many acquittals he soon was being asked to try a case nearly every day. "This activity won me no recommendations," he said later. "On the contrary, my immediate superior suggested that on account of it I was a nuisance and should be demoted." But with his promised captaincy already suspended by the Armistice, Willkie wasn't too concerned. For the first time since the Army had taken him from the profession to which he would soon return, he was a working lawyer, and the courts-martial added to his practical trial experience that had been interrupted by the war.

Before leaving Europe he wanted to visit Paris, but the Army had issued an order that no leaves were to be granted to men who hadn't served in France for six months, and that no passes were to be issued at all for sightseeing jaunts to the French capital. Despite the orders, Willkie got a friend to win leave for both of them on "official business" that would take them to a town just north of Paris. That allowed them to travel through the city, and once they reached Paris he talked the military police into letting them stay instead of going on to the destination written on their pass. He and his friend crowded as much of Paris as they could into a three-day visit and then made a wide round trip that took them to Nice and even across the border for a brief look at Northern Italy before they raced back to camp. When they arrived, they discovered the regiment had been ordered to move out and they had come within hours of being left behind.

Willkie sailed for home aboard the *Antigone* on February 15, 1919. Edith was waiting for him at the dock when the ship reached Newport News, Virginia, and he was honorably discharged from the Army on February 28. His division commander recommended him for appointment to the regular Army at the time of his discharge as "an efficient and excellent officer I would be glad to have in my command," but Willkie had seen enough of Army life.

Chapter Seven

WENDELL WILLKIE might have become a college professor, a candidate for Congress, or just another small-town lawyer when he came home from the war. Those were the opportunities that seemed most promising, but like so many other returning soldiers he wasn't sure what he wanted to do.

His father hoped he would stay in Elwood as a member of the family law firm, but his mother was against that because she thought he could do better somewhere else. Ernest H. Lindley, who had been one of his professors at Indiana University, had become president of the University of Idaho and he offered Willkie a position on his law school faculty, but the job wouldn't be available for some time and, as an unemployed civilian with a wife to support, Willkie couldn't wait. The chance to start a political career came from Madison County Democratic leader Dale Crittenberger who urged him to seek the party's nomination as a candidate for Representative from the Eighth Congressional District. That tempted Willkie most, and he decided to talk it over with

66

Frank Dailey, an Indianapolis lawyer and politician and longtime family friend.

"Sure, you might win one election on the strength of your war record," Dailey told him, "but it's normally a Republican district and one term is probably all you would get. You'd come back a small-time political has-been whose career was finished except for hanging around the county seat as a legal hack."

Dailey had a suggestion of his own. He had connections with the Firestone Tire and Rubber Company in Akron, Ohio, and happened to know the company was looking for a young lawyer to take charge of a new legal counseling service for employees. Dailey wrote a letter of recommendation, and Willkie went to Akron to look over the situation. He found the city booming in a way that reminded him of Elwood when he was a boy, but bigger and more exciting. Everywhere he looked there were busy factories, swelling housing developments, new businesses. From the newspapers he learned that Akron would turn out half a billion dollars worth of products that year, and that in a single day permits had been issued for buildings valued at more than a million dollars. He sensed an almost buccaneering spirit of economic adventure in the men to whom he spoke.

He went home and told Edith he wanted the job if he could get it, and in his formal application he wrote of his "great desire to become connected with the corporation." His personal savings were down to a hundred dollars by the time he was hired at a starting salary of $2,500 a year. He and Edith agreed that she would stay in Indiana until he was settled in the new position and he took off for Akron, found himself an inexpensive rooming house, and started work for Firestone on May 16, 1919.

Willkie was excited by the whole pattern for success he found in booming Akron, the process of corporate empire-building, the freedom of enterprise, industrial progress and expansion. It was the coming age of the tin lizzie, and of rubber tires for it, of pioneering aviation, big spending, and financial speculation; and he accepted the premise of the times that what was good for business should be good for everybody. He wanted to make something of himself and to make money.

But for all his enthusiasm for the flourishing industrial adventures that surrounded him, his starting work at Firestone turned out to be more routine than challenging. Hundreds of company workers came to him for free legal advice about small debts, threats by creditors to attach their wages, quarrels with landlords, and for help with such things as mortgages, deeds, and the writing of wills. Yet he made the service so popular with employees that the company gave him a raise within two months, another raise two months later, and a third one by the end of 1919, boosting his pay well above $5,000.

He had still more reason to celebrate his good fortune that fall with the news that he was about to become a father. On December 7, 1919, his son Philip was born, and Edith and the baby soon came to join him in Akron. For a time they shared a small apartment with another young couple, the Hubert Hannas, and later were able to buy a modest home of their own in which they lived the rest of the years they were in Ohio.

They lived frugally and Willkie put aside some money. He and a few other men pooled their funds to invest in a small piece of land in South Akron. The boom was at its height and they sold it at a good profit. With that as capital, they began speculating in real estate, buying more lots and selling them. Within months, Willkie's share had reached the heady total of $30,000. He had made the acquaintance of several officials high up in the Firestone organization and one of them passed along a tip that the company's stock was about to triple in value. Willkie invested not only all his $30,000 but borrowed even more than that to add to it in the hope of making a market killing that would bring him nearly $200,000.

He had every reason to be optimistic in the spring of 1920. Only about a year out of the Army, he had become a happily settled family man, succeeding in his chosen career and looking forward to an apparently rosy financial future. But if he had few problems of his own, those of the nation troubled him. The Senate had rejected the League of Nations. President Wilson's own stubborn refusal to seek the cooperation of Republicans, and the determination of the Republican leadership in Congress to destroy him and the Democrats politically had turned the search for peace into a battle for political power.

President Wilson, heartsick and with his health broken by the strain, had carried his fight to the people, warning that if the League were beaten or crippled by Senate amendments, "I can predict with absolute certainty that within another generation there will be another world war." After forty speeches across the nation, he collapsed. From his sickroom at the White House, the stricken President still stubbornly insisted that he would never accept any of the Republican changes and that Congress had to vote for the League as he had planned it—or nothing. The Senate had voted for nothing, rejected the treaty, and sent it back to him unapproved.

Willkie, with his devotion to Wilson's ideals and his belief in the League of Nations, threw himself into the 1920 political campaign. He delivered, as he said, "a thousand speeches" in appeals to Akron's voters to save the League by electing that year's Democratic candidate for President, the governor of their own state of Ohio, James M. Cox. With a group of other young lawyers, he sparked a Young Men's

Democratic Club into action, commandeered a small fleet of trucks, and rolled them out to Akron's street corners to serve as speaking platforms to carry "the League's banner high." He himself spoke not only from the touring trucks but to every civic club that would listen.

Cox and his running mate for vice-president, young Assistant Secretary of the Navy Franklin D. Roosevelt, campaigned vigorously to make the election a "solemn referendum" on the question of American entry into the League. But the Republicans, led by another Ohioan, Senator Warren G. Harding, straddled the issue and though they were mainly against the League took no clear stand on it. The nation's war-weary voters, wanting to throw off their cares and enjoy prosperity, decided in November to follow Harding "back to normalcy" and elected him by the largest plurality ever given any candidate for president up until that time.

Although Willkie's Democrats were defeated, he never stopped championing the cause of world cooperation, which was to become the most important mission of his life. His 1920 campaign activities brought him to Akron's attention and into close association with Governor Cox and with another of Ohio's prominent Democratic statesmen, Newton D. Baker, the pacifist former mayor of Cleveland who had directed America's wartime forces as President Wilson's Secretary of War. Cox recalled in later years that when he first became acquainted with Willkie, who introduced him at a giant campaign rally at the Akron Armory, he was "just a promising young lawyer, but even then a very commanding personality."

With the election over, Willkie came to a career decision he had been debating for some time. He had done well with Firestone but the limiting work offered little opportunity for the experience he wanted as an attorney. There was a position open in the well-established law firm of Mather and

Nesbitt, and although taking it would mean temporarily cutting his salary almost in half, his stock market investments seemed security enough against immediate financial worries. Edith agreed that he should make the change and he turned in his resignation.

Firestone officials tried to persuade him not to leave and finally Harvey Firestone himself called Willkie into his office for a conference and offered him $10,000 a year to stay with the company. Willkie answered that he was sorry but that his mind was made up. "I like you, young man," the rubber magnate told him in parting, "but I don't think you will ever amount to a great deal." When Willkie asked why not, Firestone said, "Because I understand you are a Democrat and no Democrat can ever amount to much."

Willkie started the new year of 1921 with Mather and Nesbitt as an assistant to Roy Nesbitt, helping to handle clients that included utility companies, banks, industries, and a major railroad. But he had hardly begun his new job when the economic recession of 1921 sent stocks spiraling downward and the Firestone shares he had bought with the hope of becoming wealthy dropped to one-fourth of what he had invested in them. His profits were wiped out, his savings were gone, and he was left some $12,000 in debt. His new job was all he had to keep him going. "I didn't survive at the bar through any love of work—I survived through the necessity of making money," he once told an interviewer. "I applied myself to the bar because I had to. Otherwise I would have starved."

He took to getting into the law office at seven in the morning, was still there late at night, and brought his lunch with him so he wouldn't have to waste time going out to eat. Friends who dropped in during the evening would find him lying on a rug on the office floor, books and papers around him, and when he did go home he took more work with him.

71

He chain-smoked cigarettes, lived in his clothes, hardly knew or cared what food was put on his plate, and was almost totally indifferent to his surroundings. Social activities and even regular family life were all but forgotten. His associates agreed that he drove himself to become what one of them called "the hardest working and fastest thinking lawyer at the local bar." His work also made him a partner in the firm, which became Mather, Nesbitt and Willkie. He had helped to increase its already profitable corporation practice to three times what it had been.

Willkie soon was the firm's chief trial lawyer, spending as many as two hundred days a year in actual courtroom activity, and working nights to prepare cases for the next day. But it wasn't only his driving energy and enormous capacity for work that brought him to prominence at the bar. He was a decidedly talented lawyer and skilled courtroom practitioner, with an actor's sense of dramatic gesture and timing, and a voice and intense manner that were powerfully convincing. A thunderer when the moment called for it, he had a reputation for "making juries swallow hard." But his usual style was easy-going, friendly and often humorous.

The courtrooms taught Willkie tactics that were to serve him well in politics. He improved his ability to think quickly on his feet, to handle himself well in the give-and-take of questions and answers, to anticipate reactions, and keep a step ahead of them. Constantly putting his arguments on public trial under the tension of different circumstances every day, he learned to appeal to all types of people in a way that would win convincing belief in what he said.

His activities in the American Legion first pushed him into greater prominence as a public speaker. The recession had put some 45,000 Akron workers out of jobs, many of them former servicemen who had come to work in the rubber factories after the war and had been left stranded. Veterans were turning to the Legion in great numbers for help with bonus and insurance applications, in seeking loans, or to get railroad fare back to the home towns they had come from. But the Legion itself was in danger of fading out of existence in Akron for lack of funds. To save the organization, Willkie helped combine nine struggling Legion posts into one. Elected commander, he went to work to raise money through various affairs that were climaxed in a concert by opera star Madame Schumann-Heink which brought the Legion three thousand dollars and finally lifted it out of debt.

Appearing at service clubs and other organizations for the Legion, Willkie began to get a reputation as an entertaining and informative public speaker. Soon he was being invited to make two or three speeches a week at all sorts of business and fraternal gatherings and at schools, churches, and nearby colleges. He loved to talk, always without a script, and seldom turned down an invitation. He spoke about the national government, local problems, business, law, banking, history, patriotism, the folly of war, education, taxes or whatever else seemed appropriate. Once he forgot what he had been invited to talk about and had to ask an official of the group what the theme of the evening's address was supposed to be. A frequent keynote speaker at Akron's patriotic exercises, he delivered eulogies of Washington, Jefferson, and Lincoln. He once played the role of Lincoln, made up as an actor to resemble the Emancipator, in a Fourth of July pageant before an audience of five thousand, and impressively recited the Emancipation Proclamation as he struck symbolic shackles from the wrists of a slave.

He had arrived in Akron without a friend in the city, unknown and almost broke, to start work at a routine legal job. Within a few years he had achieved a high place in his profession, had become a well-known community figure, and had dozens of friends on every level of Akron's business and social life. He had worked hard but in most things he had insisted upon going his own way and being himself, less a rebel than he once was, perhaps, but certainly not a conformist. Outside Akron he was still unknown but he had begun to attract the attention of some very important men.

Chapter Eight

WENDELL WILLKIE had an inside view of the strategy of national politics when he was elected as a delegate from Akron to the Democratic National Convention in New York in 1924. Newton D. Baker had asked him to serve as his political lieutenant in a fight to keep the party's support of the League of Nations alive. Willkie told his Akron supporters that he also meant to wage another convention battle to help "put the Democratic party on record against the Ku Klux Klan."

The 1924 convention, held in the sweltering June heat of New York's old Madison Square Garden, was one of the most tempestuous in the party's history, a bitter spectacle of fiercely divided interests that were locked in debates and quarrels that went on for days. Willkie worked closely with Baker and also with Governor Cox, both of whom were among secondary contenders for the presidential nomination. He sat in on the maneuvering that goes on behind the scenes in the writing of a platform and the choice of a candidate, and gained first-hand knowledge of the political facts of life, which left him somewhat disillusioned.

75

William Jennings Bryan, his father's old friend, was there and Willkie remembered him as the spellbinder of his childhood, but Bryan had become an unwelcome ghost of the past with his party influence gone. When Bryan attempted to speak, his once peerless voice only an echo of what it had been, delegates embarrassed him into silence by shouting, "Louder!" Bryan left the convention and went back to his hotel room to listen to its decisions by radio, the new device that was letting the whole nation hear the proceedings.

What the nation heard was only part of the battles that went on in the smoke-filled rooms over the issues of the Klan, the League, and Prohibition. The Klan, resurrected from Civil War days, was regaining strength not only in the South but in other parts of the nation and especially in sections of Indiana and Ohio where it was spreading its doctrines of racial and religious hatred. Some politicians sympathized with it and some feared to stand against it. Convention delegates who favored the Klan were heatedly opposed to New York's Governor Alfred E. Smith, one of the leaders in the race for the presidential nomination, who happened to be a Catholic and who had denounced the Klan and wanted the party to go on record against it. Smith, who had the backing of most eastern and big-city delegates, also urged the repeal of Prohibition.

An almost equal number of delegates were determined to give the nomination to California's William G. McAdoo, former Secretary of the Treasury and Wilson's son-in-law, whose supporters included many from Midwestern and rural areas as well as Klan sympathizers and who hated everything Smith was and stood for and were firmly in favor of Prohibition. The Democrats started their convention in a jubilant mood, supremely hopeful they could choose a candidate who would sweep them to victory over the Republicans in the coming election following the collapse of the Harding

76

administration in graft and scandal. But it soon became obvious that they were hopelessly deadlocked and would have trouble nominating anybody.

Willkie's stand against the Klan, favoring the writing of a party platform resolution that would denounce it by name, aroused the rage of Klan leaders in Akron and they sent him a telegram, intending to intimidate him by asking, "When did you join the payroll of the Pope?" He shot back an answer: "The Klan can go to hell." But the convention refused by a single vote to write the plank into the platform, and Willkie had to content himself with finding a sense of victory in the close decision. "The fact that the resolution was defeated by only one vote means that the Klan was absolutely exposed," he told reporters. "They didn't gain anything by keeping the name of the Klan out of the plank. It got just as much publicity. I consider that there was an absolute repudiation of the Klan by the convention."

He couldn't take that much consolation from the convention's failure to endorse the League of Nations. What happened left him heartsick, and he had strong feelings about it all his life. The Resolutions Committee argued the question for five days and nights as Newton Baker led the fight to get the Democrats to endorse the League without qualification. Twenty years afterwards, Willkie wrote: "I shall never forget those early morning hours when Baker, physically a slight man, would return exhausted to his room to tell us— ardent, young and uninitiated in the obduracy of mentally-set politicians—of his battles in the committtees and to get fresh stimulation from our naïve and infectious belief that so just a cause, so ably advocated, could not lose."

But opponents of the League resolution killed it in committee on the political grounds that the issue was a dead one that wouldn't win any votes. Baker's speech in pleading for the League was one Willkie emotionally called "not only the greatest speech in the country but the greatest speech in the world." Willkie said, "I saw hard, stern men cry during the plea for the issue, a plea against war." In his plea, Baker denounced the talk about "expediency and votes" and said, "I am talking about life and death and love and duty." But he lost the fight not only in the committee, but also when he carried it directly to the convention floor.

The man Willkie blamed most for failing to support Baker's fight to endorse the League of Nations was Franklin D. Roosevelt. A strong advocate of the League as the vice-presidential candidate of the election before, Roosevelt was accused by Willkie of being among those who took the side of expediency in 1924 because the resolution would be a politically unattractive plank in the party platform. Willkie afterwards charged that the "fight for international cooperation" was lost "largely because the New York delegation, under the leadership of Franklin D. Roosevelt and others, voted two to one against it." Willkie would face the demands of political expediency himself in the years ahead but he hadn't then learned that compromise sometimes is forced upon all politicians. The League was close to his heart, and that first impression of Roosevelt always stayed in his mind and made him forever cautious in his dealings with the man he both fought and learned to admire.

In 1924, Roosevelt was returning to politics after winning his personal battle against infantile paralysis and was the spokesman for Al Smith, whom Willkie also backed because Smith "was against the Klan." Roosevelt scored a great personal triumph at the convention with his speech nominating Smith as the man who should become the "happy warrior" of the Democrats, an address that was praised by others as "the most perfect nominating speech ever given" and one that helped bring Roosevelt back into top position among party leaders. But Willkie, who talked freely to reporters about everything else that happened at the convention, had no comment to make about Roosevelt's speech.

When the convention balloting began, the deadlock between Smith and McAdoo made it likely that some compromise candidate would be chosen, and the Ohio delegation first supported Cox then switched to Baker. After seventy-four roll calls had been taken, Willkie made the move to release the Ohio delegation from support of its "favorite sons" and worked to swing the Ohio vote solidly to Smith. When Smith received votes from only about half the Ohio delegates, Willkie charged that some Ohioans seemed to be afraid of the "goblins of the Klan." The stormy convention fight to choose a candidate went on for nine wearying days. On the ninety-first ballot, Willkie switched from Smith to conservative corporation lawyer and former ambassador John W. Davis. When Smith and McAdoo finally agreed to withdraw, Davis was nominated by the exhausted delegates who had taken 103 votes to reach a compromise.

After Willkie returned to Akron, he told a reporter that "with John W. Davis and Calvin Coolidge in leadership of the two great parties we will have an able and dignified presentation and analysis of the issues." He thought the vital questions to be decided were the influence of the Klan on public office, the League of Nations, and tax reduction. But "Silent Cal" Coolidge kept mostly silent on controversial issues, Davis was hurt because many rural voters associated him with the financial barons of Wall Street, and a nation still enjoying prosperity and unmoved by the revelations of the Harding scandals voted overwhelmingly in November to "Keep Cool with Coolidge."

Willkie waged his own political war against the Klan in Akron, and in 1925 led a "citizens' crusade" to prevent the Klan from controlling the public schools. The head of Akron's Board of Education was the Exalted Cyclops of the

79

Summit County Klan, and three board members also belonged to the Klan and voted as a majority on school board decisions. Three other members of the board resigned, charging that the Klan was dictating the policies of the city's schools. Willkie organized a meeting of one hundred prominent citizens "to keep politics out of the schools," and they formed what was called the non-Political Public School League.

The Klan's leader, Willkie told the meeting, "has thrown down the challenge that he controls this city. I do not think he does. I think that if we properly organize and fight that the people who believe in the American form of government are in sufficient number that we can elect four members to the Board of Education who will express the true selection of this city." He was named to a committee to nominate anti-Klan candidates. That November, the committee's candidates, including a close friend of Willkie's, lawyer Robert Guinther, were elected. The Akron *Beacon Journal* predicted that the school board victory foreshadowed the end of the Klan's power in Akron, and Willkie's citizens' group was credited with leading "the only political fight in which endorsements of the hooded order have been smashed since the organization of that order in this city."

When Willkie wasn't busy with civic affairs or at the office, he usually could be found reading a book, and his Akron home began to overflow with them as had his boyhood home in Elwood. He and Edith sometimes had a few close friends in for the evening, but they hardly ever gave large parties or dinners, and seldom went to them. They shunned most outside entertainment and what he called "social trivialities." He felt there were more important things to do with the little free time he had.

He was an affectionate if somewhat absent-minded husband and father. Knowing his tendency to ignore time,

80

Edith made a habit of keeping the household clocks turned a bit ahead, and he once jokingly complained that he had spent much of his life "in a state of chronological inaccuracy." When he needed a new hat she would buy it and substitute it for the one he had been wearing, and it was she who talked him into buying new suits and insisted upon his getting a haircut. She also did her best to see that his clothes were neatly pressed, although they still looked rumpled an hour or so after he had put them on because of his habit of sprawling over furniture, sitting on a desk corner, a packing box, the floor, or whatever other perch might be available. He had almost no interest in food, furnishings, or appearances.

All their friends agreed that they seemed happily married and devoted even though Willkie's life increasingly centered around interests outside his home. Edith tolerantly overlooked the fact that he never remembered anniversaries. "I think it is nice when men remember birthday and wedding anniversaries, but it is not important," she once said. "The really important thing is how they treat you every day." She smilingly added, "I have no complaints." She kept him comfortable, managed the household so he never had to be troubled with minor domestic problems, and if she was lonely at times because he worked longer hours than most husbands and wasn't interested in the social affairs enjoyed by most of their friends, she also said, "I can find more pleasure in just walking down the street with Wendell than in anything else I know."

In a letter to a friend, Willkie humorously characterized himself as "a restless and altogether unsatisfactory husband" and said it had been his good fortune to "marry a sane Indiana girl with the rare capacity to bear with my faults." As a father, he treated his son with somewhat the same attitudes toward learning and experience as his father had

81

shown him. He wanted Philip to be self-reliant, inquisitive and independent in his thinking, and sometimes mildly complained that Edith was too protective, but they had no serious differences about Philip's upbringing.

Outside his home and office Willkie had what a friend called "almost an obsession" to talk to all sorts of people, as though he wanted to draw out the ideas and opinions of everybody in town. He belonged to the University Club, the Exchange Club and the Akron City Club but avoided club politics and most meetings, and used the clubs mainly as places where he could go to find a good friendly argument. At the suggestion of his law partners he also reluctantly joined the rather exclusive Portage Country Club and sometimes sat around the locker room joking with golfers about their scores, but he had no interest in the game itself. Even fishing, which he had enjoyed as a boy, apparently bored him as a man. He went on fishing trips now and then with friends from Akron but they said he preferred to sit and read while a guide caught the fish.

Willkie had become financially secure and he began investing money in stock of the Ohio State Bank, one of his law firm's clients, which seemed much safer to him than the stock market after the lesson he had learned trying to make a quick killing in Firestone stock. He was named to the bank's board of directors and later became a director of one of the utility companies handled by his firm, the Northern Ohio Power and Light Company. Acting for the company, he appeared before the state public utility commission to negotiate new franchises and changes in rate schedules, but he denied the charge later made by political enemies that his main job in Akron was as a power company lobbyist to influence decisions that benefitted the company at the cost of consumers.

Willkie's interests as a lawyer turned from the courtrooms

to the complex structure of large corporations. His success in his profession and the respect other lawyers had for him were confirmed early in March, 1925 when, at the age of thirty-three, he was unanimously elected president of the Akron Bar Association, the youngest president the Association ever had. That July, the Akron *Beacon Journal* published Willkie's photograph and an account of his civic achievements among those of a group of some seventy citizens "prominent in the development of Akron."

Among those who had become interested in Willkie's abilities was utility magnate Bernard Capen Cobb. Northern Ohio Power and Light, later to become Ohio Edison, was one of many utilities Cobb was forming into a giant corporation, and in 1926 he sent through a memorandum: "We should not let Willkie get away from us. He is a comer and we should keep an eye on him."

Cobb was busy organizing what was to become the Commonwealth and Southern Corporation, the billion-dollar holding company at the top of a mammoth combine of other utility companies. Backed by New York financial houses, it controlled the voting stock of a system that at one point furnished electricity, gas, transportation, and other utilities through 165 companies to several thousand communities in nearly one-fourth of the nation's industrial and farm states. As Cobb unified the web-like system of operating companies, he decided its legal policies should be directed from one New York office and in 1929 he offered the job to Willkie.

But at first Willkie wasn't too eager to accept. Akron had given him what he called "the happiest and most satisfying years of my life." He had a good home, good friends, a sense of belonging to the community, and had achieved prominence in civic, business, and financial circles. He thought his personal life was more rewarding in Akron than it would be in New York. "I was well-fixed," he said. "I expected to stay in Akron the rest of my life."

The offer to become chief attorney for a giant corporation was flattering and he knew it might lead to even greater opportunities. He had been promised a starting salary of $36,000 a year, nearly a third more than his income as a lawyer in Akron, but his personal tastes were simple and he already had enough money for anything he wanted to buy. What seemed far more important to him was his freedom to do as he pleased and to speak his own mind. He feared that working for a big corporation would mean carrying out policies made by those higher up and that he no longer would be his own boss.

He went to Chicago to talk it over with his old friend and former roommate at Indiana University, Maurice Bluhm, who had become an attorney for a large railroad. In Akron he talked to lawyer friends about the "terrible decision" he had to make. They told him they thought he would be crazy to turn down what was the chance of a lifetime. But still he hesitated, and said to them, "But will I be free?"

Finally on August 8, 1929, he announced that he was resigning from his Akron law firm to become associated with John C. Weadock in a New York firm to be known as Weadock & Willkie, which would be the legal representative of the new Commonwealth and Southern Corporation. "The most difficult thing I ever had to do is leave Akron," he told the members of the Bar Association at a farewell dinner given in his honor. "I never would have considered leaving if I had realized it would be so hard to sever my associations here."

Years afterwards, when he had achieved national fame, Willkie wrote to a friend: "I sometimes wonder whether I have lived on in as much ease and contentment as I would have lived if I had stayed."

Chapter Nine

THE stock tickers of Wall Street were still tapping out a record of golden wealth when Wendell Willkie arrived in New York to take charge of the legal affairs of Commonwealth and Southern Corporation on October 1, 1929. But despite optimistic predictions that prosperity would go on forever, Willkie had a strong premonition that the get-rich-quick boom was about over. He told his wife, "Billie, we've come too late."

Twenty-nine days later, the bottom dropped out of the market. On the Black Tuesday of October 29, in a bedlam of near-hysteria, investors dumped some sixteen million shares on the floor of the Stock Exchange, and the greatest selling wave in history touched off a panic that wiped out thirty billion dollars in paper profits. Despair gradually replaced the hope that returning prosperity was "just around the corner" and the great depression fastened its years of hardship upon the land. Commonwealth and Southern's common stock dropped in value to less than two dollars a share, and the corporation's gross earnings declined at an average rate of more than a million dollars a month as slackening business lowered demands for electric power.

Willkie himself lost heavily in the crash. Like many others he had thought he was being wise to put his savings into Ohio bank stock rather than into more speculative stocks. But the depression forced the bank to close, and under Ohio law Willkie became liable for twice the listed value of the stock he owned. He found himself several hundred thousand dollars in debt and was still paying off assessments on it ten years later.

"In the money-mad period of the Twenties the heads of some of our corporations forgot their primary function—that of running a business enterprise in a way that would be sound for the worker, the consumer and the investor," he said afterwards, looking back at those years. "Instead of attending to the duties of management they began playing with corporate structures as with a child's building blocks, becoming promoters rather than business men. And some financiers in Wall Street and elsewhere, instead of serving as a link between the savings of the people and the enormous capital needs of industry, became jugglers of finance, concerned primarily with making money and securing power for themselves."

With factories shutting down, businesses going bankrupt, banks closing their doors, and millions thrown out of work, many Americans blamed big business for all their woes and looked upon its doings with suspicion. Some utility companies had earned the industry a bad reputation through pyramiding finances, corruption of public officials, and huge slush funds to buy influence. Sensational headlines produced by congressional investigations blackened the industry more, and the scandals soon were to be topped by the dramatic collapse of the giant utility empire created by Samuel Insull, at a loss to investors of millions of dollars.

Willkie had been right in predicting the end of easy-money prosperity but wrong in thinking he had arrived in New York too late for his own success. The depression and the conditions it created gave him his opportunity, and made him a national figure. He had come to the utility industry when it needed housecleaning and reform. Even more, it needed a defender who wasn't blind to its faults but who believed that liberal-minded management could correct them.

His work as attorney for Commonwealth and Southern involved him in all its activities and gave him a top-level knowledge of the utility business and corporation management. Bernard Cobb, who had brought him to New York, was more than pleased by the efficient way Willkie got things done and gradually relieved him of most of his legal duties to make him his management assistant. Willkie helped Cobb reorganize Commonwealth and Southern to cut down its superstructure of interlocking stock companies and to consolidate the operating companies that actually produced power for consumers.

Soon there were rumors that Cobb, who was in ill health, was grooming Willkie as his successor. On January 24, 1933, as he was about to celebrate his forty-first birthday, Willkie became president of Commonwealth and Southern at a salary of $75,000 a year. He later refused an offer by the directors to increase his salary with the comment that he was being paid as much as the President of the United States, and that was enough. Although he held complete authority as Commonwealth and Southern's chief executive, he didn't want the formal title of Chairman of the Board tacked to his name and he abolished the position. "It's too stuffy," he said. "I would have to be too dignified."

In his habits and attitudes he seemed unimpressed by the fact that he had become a big business tycoon. He had moved his family into an apartment on Fifth Avenue near Central Park, a fashionable residence but not as luxurious as he could have afforded. When it was suggested that he might enjoy the richer surroundings of a home in the suburbs, he shrugged off the idea with the answer that he was perfectly comfortable where he was and didn't intend to waste his time as a club car commuter. His home life was as casual as his indifference to clocks, meals, and set routines always had made it. He still sprawled with his long legs over the arm of any handy chair, forgot to lock the apartment door behind him when he breezed out in a hurry, and wore whatever clothes he happened to pull from the closet.

The apartment was filled with books, often left open to some passage he had been reading in the bedroom, kitchen, or bath. Mrs. Willkie liked to tell about how they once had an interior decorator come to look at the apartment with the thought of redecorating it. Appalled by the sight of so many helter-skelter volumes, the decorator patronizingly remarked, "Books just aren't being used much these days, you know. We'll have to get rid of them to do the place properly." Willkie overheard the conversation and that was the end of plans to redecorate the apartment. When he had nothing else to read he would dip into dictionaries and encyclopedias, and whether at home or traveling he consumed newspapers by the armful and seldom passed a newsstand without picking up the latest editions.

He had the use of a chauffeur-driven automobile but preferred to ride the subway or to hop into a taxi when he was in a hurry to get to his office in the downtown financial district. When he had the time, he enjoyed walking around midtown Manhattan, but when lost in his thoughts sometimes failed to notice it was raining, and frequently turned corners in the wrong direction. Willkie was of the opinion that nobody ever accomplished much working only forty or fifty hours a week, and he liked to arrive at his office long before anyone else in the morning so as to get as much work done as he could before the usual interruptions began. He continued to spend many nights, weekends, and holidays at the office and said those were the best times for work because there was nobody around to bother him.

While he certainly had no contempt for wealth and was pleased by his own financial success, he felt that having money was no particular measure of the man who had it. He wrote to a college student who sought his advice about a career that while money had its value in giving a man greater independence to do the things he wished to do, he did not believe the pursuit of it "has the slightest to do with either happiness or satisfaction in life." He considered a good education the best thing money could buy and quietly provided funds to help at least forty boys through college.

Despite the pressures of work, he found some time to relax with his family and enjoy his teen-aged son's companionship. The Willkies took many short family trips together, and he often took Philip along on his habitual sightseeing visits to historic places. They vacationed in Bermuda the summer of 1930, had a place in the Adirondacks the next summer, and spent a full month together in Europe the following year. With his brother Edward, who was working in Europe, Willkie went on an automobile tour of Belgium and Luxembourg. He took Philip and Mrs. Willkie to see the Chicago World's Fair in 1933, and in other years vacationed in Puerto Rico and in Michigan.

His father died on November 27, 1930, and although it wasn't unexpected, since Herman Willkie had long been suffering from cancer, his death was a severe emotional loss. Right up to his father's final years, Willkie sought his opinion on important personal decisions, sometimes phoned him to talk out legal problems, and there had been a lively ex-

89

change of letters between them to discuss books and ideas. After the funeral services in Elwood, Willkie decided the epitaph on his father's gravestone should read: "He devoted his life to his children." And after Willkie had become famous, he said that at times when he was tempted to get swell-headed over something he only had to remember that his father had been "a bigger man than I will ever be." In a letter to an Elwood acquaintance he wrote: "My father's memory is a religion to me."

All of Willkie's brothers and sisters were drawn by various interests to foreign lands, and for a time he was the only one left in the United States. Julia was an industrial bacteriologist in Canada, Bob an Army major in the Philippines, Edward a packing company executive in Belgium, and Fred a distilling company vice president in charge of constructing new plants in Scotland. Charlotte, the wife of Edward's former Annapolis roommate Captain Paul Pihl, was with her husband in Hawaii where he was stationed by the Navy before becoming an attaché of the American embassy in Berlin. Despite the distances that separated them, they remained a close-knit family in their free exchange by letter of problems and advice, and in the interest they took in each other's activities. Willkie wrote to Julia of Philip's school achievements and of his plans to enter Princeton, and in letters to his brother Edward suggested letting Philip make a long pre-college tour of Europe, but instead finally arranged for Philip to take a six-weeks' course at Heidelberg University.

Much of Willkie's family life began to center around the farms he bought in Indiana, which he came to think of as more his real home than the apartment in New York. He bought the first one, a 350-acre tract near his wife's home town of Rushville, in January 1935, and added neighboring farms through the years until he owned about sixteen hundred acres. He considered them an investment for his own and his family's future, not a rich man's hobby, and he ran them to make a profit, sharing on a fifty-fifty basis with the tenants who lived on them, raising hogs and cattle. Willkie turned his early profits back into building up and improving the properties but after that, they were self-supporting and brought a good income both to him and to his tenants. Willkie's father-in-law, Philip Wilk, whose business was hit by the depression, ran the farms at first and when he died, Willkie shocked the farm community by asking librarian Mary Sleeth, Edith's longtime friend, to take over as manager. When he first suggested the idea she said, "People will think you're crazy, having a woman manage your farms." He told her: "I got where I am by doing things other people thought were crazy."

Finally persuaded, she took over and the farms prospered under her management. As frequently as he could, Willkie flew from wherever he was for weekends, vacations, and brief holidays in Rushville. He got to know his tenants well and some of them became good personal friends, but his business arrangements with them were definite and he insisted upon full and regular reports from every farm. Christmas in Rushville with Philip and Mrs. Willkie became a fixed family tradition and the farms became the place to which he always could escape to restore his energies, walking the fields and being close to the earth. He once said he wished he had nothing to do but sit all day on a hillside looking at the trees and watching the cattle graze.

But as chief executive of Commonwealth and Southern, he seldom had a chance to sit long anywhere. He spent an average of one hundred days a year on the road, inspecting plants of the power system that spread from North to South over eleven states, conferring with company officials to iron out special problems and to make decisions about rates, fi-

91

nancing, and operations. When he set out from his New York office for some area, up to a dozen company experts and power technicians would travel with him in a small motorcade of automobiles. Willkie visited not only big-city headquarters of his companies but at one time or another nearly all the hundreds of smaller communities they served. He had his own method of gaining first-hand knowledge about any community that was new to him. When he arrived in town, he would go first to see the local newspaper editor, then to the town library, next to the Chamber of Commerce, and finally to the superintendent of schools. In that way, he felt he could get some quick knowledge of local conditions so he could make intelligent decisions on company policy for that community.

He made sweeping changes in the corporation itself. Determined to clean house, put the system on a solid operating basis and boost its income, he started by writing off more than half a billion dollars in so-called "watered stocks" that had been given a higher book value than the actual assets they represented. He shook up the board of directors and replaced the bankers on the board with men who headed operating companies so the corporation would be under the control of those who produced its power instead of the money men. And at a time when most of the industry held that rate cuts were impossible, he cut his rates, extended company services, and worked out a "bonus plan" so that consumers who used more electricity would receive some of it free.

The depression had about knocked the bottom out of the sale of electric appliances, on which the household use of electricity depended, and other companies were firing salesmen and cutting their advertising and promotion staffs. Willkie hired hundreds of additional salesmen for an aggressive campaign to push the sale of appliances. He liberalized credit terms, told every employee of Commonwealth and Southern from the top down to get out and sell, and set an example himself by becoming what he later jokingly boasted was "the world's best gadget salesman." His staff said it was no idle boast. During the worst of the depression he sold appliances in the poorest parts of the country. He traveled over the entire system to launch appliance sales drives in big cities and small towns, to give pep talks to salesmen and local utility officials, and to push the merchandising with groups of housewives, merchants, and farmers.

He did such a good job of whipping up the enthusiasm of his own employees that when he arrived unrecognized at one of his utility plants, a receptionist tried to sell him a toaster, and at another place an elevator operator tried to convince him he should buy a new refrigerator. Appliance sales zoomed to four times what they had been. The sale of electricity by Commonwealth and Southern subsidiaries more than doubled. Because of the expanding sales and services, the corporation was able to reduce its power rates until they were thirty-seven per cent below the industry average for the United States.

During the years he was so busy running his corporation, Willkie also was waging a fight for public opinion that brought him into a running battle with the government, Congress and the President of the United States. He began it to defend the interests of his company and its stockholders, but it became a political crusade to drive Franklin D. Roosevelt from the White House and to take his place.

Chapter Ten

PROBABLY the last man Wendell Willkie wanted the Democrats to nominate for President in 1932 was Franklin D. Roosevelt. He wasn't against Roosevelt's call for sweeping social and economic reforms to lift the country out of the Depression, but his own candidate for the nomination was still the man he had backed in 1924, Newton D. Baker.

Willkie went to the Democratic National Convention in Chicago in June 1932 to work on Baker's team, as he had eight years before, because he felt that Baker, as he put it, "almost alone through the isolationist 1920's fought consistently for world cooperation." Mankind's greatest need, Willkie unwaveringly believed, was for some international organization such as Woodrow Wilson's League of Nations, and he still blamed Roosevelt, rightly or not, for failing to support Baker's fight in 1924 to revive the League as part of the Democratic party platform.

He hoped that a convention deadlock might give Baker at least a slim chance to win the nomination. But when the deadlock came, Baker and half a dozen other contenders were quickly squeezed out of the running, and the struggle

94

for ballots became a showdown between Roosevelt and Alfred E. Smith. Formerly the closest of political allies, Roosevelt and Smith had parted in a fight for control of the Democratic Party in New York, and Willkie favored Smith.

Further disillusioned by the political maneuvering of the Roosevelt forces at the Convention, Willkie was far from enthusiastic when Roosevelt emerged as the chosen candidate. His attitude toward the whole Convention had become somewhat dampened by the time Roosevelt made the stirring acceptance speech in which he declared, "I pledge you, I pledge myself, to a new deal for the American people."

Disappointed that Baker wasn't the candidate instead of Roosevelt, Willkie went on to Rushville for a visit and told his father-in-law, Philip Wilk, that he supposed he had seen "history in the making" in Chicago but "it isn't the way they tell it in the books." Still, Willkie did approve the Democratic platform upon which Roosevelt stood for election in 1932 and he contributed to the campaign, and as a loyal Democrat voted that November to help put Roosevelt in the White House.

In New York, Willkie became a member of the party's First District Club and a contributor to local campaigns, but he took no part in national Democratic activities after 1932. However, he was among those elected from the Tammany-controlled district to the County Democratic Committtee along with Roosevelt's campaign manager, James A. Farley, and Democratic National Committee Treasurer, Frank C. Walker, who later would succeed Farley as Postmaster General in the Roosevelt cabinet.

Willkie remained a Democrat through six years of fighting the power policies of the Roosevelt administration even after he had turned to attack its whole philosophy of government. But as a Democrat, he also remained a middle-of-the-road

95

moderate, still a follower of Wilson's New Freedom more than Roosevelt's New Deal. He attacked the New Deal not because of its social goals but because he felt that its spreading agencies were growing into a giant bureaucracy that threatened to rule the nation by self-assumed authority. In the beginning, his stand was less political. He was simply a business executive who fought to save his business and his company's profits.

Franklin D. Roosevelt became President of the United States less than a month after Willkie became head of Commonwealth and Southern, and one of the first agencies set up under the New Deal to combat the Depression was the Tennessee Valley Authority. Sponsored in Congress by Senator George Norris of Nebraska, long a foe of utility companies and an advocate of government-produced power for public use, the TVA brought to reality a huge development plan Norris had fought for since the Harding administration.

The TVA, which eventually became one of the great and permanent achievements of the New Deal, called for a bold new experiment in public planning to harness the power of the mighty Tennessee River, lost for years in destructive floods and waste, and turn it to the social and economic benefit of the nearly five million people who lived in its valley. It was planned to halt the floods and restore millions of acres of eroded land to productive use, to bring electricity to half a million homes and businesses, to lighten the burdens of farmers and their families and to start the wheels of new industries turning, to open the river to new commerce, and to lift the vast area out of its bankrupt past. The TVA's planners envisioned its effect upon the people of the valley in giving them hope and ambition that would lead to better homes, improved schools, and a whole new status of well-being, and would help end the ravages of poverty, ignorance, and disease.

But the key to the entire plan was the electric power that would come from the construction of great flood-control dams along the river and its tributaries, and that meant the Government would be in direct competition with utility companies in the production, sale, and distribution of electricity. The Government would build and own power plants and transmission lines, duplicate the services of private business, and cut the profits of established companies. The TVA's opponents charged that this was unfair competition and they also feared it might be the start of a gradual Government attempt to convert the whole nation to public power and put the multi-billion dollar industry out of existence.

Four of Willkie's companies were in the area directly involved in the TVA plan, and he was forced to take the leadership in a controversy that would rage through the 1930's in newspapers and magazines, on radio, and in the halls of government. Not that he didn't thoroughly enjoy what became the biggest argument of his life. Without it, he never would have gained the national attention that made him a famous man and propelled him into the race for the presidency. But he had no political ambitions when he started the fight to save his companies, which happened merely by the fact of geography to lie within the path of a New Deal dream.

Willkie hurried to Washington before the bill was passed to testify against it in April, 1933 at hearings of the House Committee on Military Affairs. He argued that "to take our markets is to take our property" and suggested that instead of duplicating services that already existed the Government should sell his companies the power it produced and let them distribute it over their lines. If Congress wouldn't do that, he said, and insisted on passing the bill as written, then it should be willing to pay the companies "fair compensation" just as it would pay farmers for land that would be flooded by the new TVA dams.

But Willkie's testimony had no effect upon a Congress eager to give President Roosevelt the legislation needed to carry out the pledges of the New Deal. The President had promised in his election campaign that he would clean up the scandal-ridden utility industry, end its long history of high rates and juggled finances, and find ways to produce cheap power for the people. In the public mind good and bad utility companies were lumped together, and many Americans looked upon all of them with distrust. The people wanted the TVA, and Congress approved it overwhelmingly.

Still hopeful that some arrangement could be worked out with the Government for his companies to buy the power produced by the new dams, Willkie went along with the project at first. But the TVA soon announced that it meant to set up its own full system, not only to provide the area with "the widest possible use of power" but also to establish a "yardstick" so that consumers everywhere in the country could measure the rates of their own local power companies against the TVA rates, to see whether the private companies were getting too much money for their electricity.

Willkie charged that the Government's "yardstick" was "all rubber" and the TVA's low rates were no measurement at all because Government subsidies and other advantages were not figured in the costs, and the Government didn't have to pay taxes as private companies did. "Whenever a householder in Tupelo, Mississippi, switches on a light," Willkie was to say, "everybody in the United States helps to pay for it."

After months of negotiation to find some sort of working agreement, at least until the TVA finished building its dams, Willkie and TVA Director David Lilienthal reached a temporary truce that set up separate areas in which Commonwealth and Southern and the TVA would not compete. Among other arrangements, the five-year agreement called for the transfer of certain Commonwealth and Southern properties, mainly in Alabama and Mississippi, to the TVA. But the contract was hardly signed before the deal was partly blocked by a group of stockholders of the Alabama Power Company. They started a court suit to prevent the transfer of their property in the hope that the TVA might be declared unconstitutional.

Meanwhile, President Roosevelt threw a real scare into the whole power industry. In a speech at Tupelo, Mississippi, in which he praised the community for being the first to buy all its power from the TVA, he declared that "what you are doing here is going to be copied in every state in the Union before we get through." He was talking about future plans to create more TVA's in other parts of the country, but to the utility companies it sounded like a threat by the government to take over their entire industry.

Up to then most of Willkie's criticisms of the TVA had been mild, and he had even praised its directors as "men of intelligence, energy and devotion," saying there was no reason for bitter exchanges over a question that should be decided on the facts alone. But he began to sharpen his tone and to hit harder and more directly, and he stepped up his speaking schedule. Because nobody else seemed willing to assume the role, he found himself in the position of defending not only his company but the whole industry. For the first time in his life what he said was carried by the national news wires, and printed in newspapers across the country as he delivered speeches at meetings of banking and financial groups in New York and other cities during the fall of 1934.

Willkie had been trying to arrange a conference with President Roosevelt to talk over the situation, and they met for the first time at the White House on December 13, 1934. The President described the meeting as "entirely amicable," and Willkie told reporters he was "very favorably impressed" with the President's attitude toward the power question. Actually, the meeting accomplished very little but it did establish a personal relationship that led to a number of other White House talks and frequent exchanges of notes and letters as Willkie and the President tried in private to reach some solution to the problems they continued to battle out in public.

In a joking telegram to his wife after his first meeting with Roosevelt, Willkie said, "I did not tell him what you think of him." But to the President himself he sent a gracious note of thanks in which he expressed the hope that not everything bad said about his companies would be believed.

Roosevelt promptly answered: "I hope you give as little credence to the statements you hear about me as I do to the many statements I hear about what you say and do."

In another exchange of letters, Willkie hoped that "certain misunderstandings can be cleared away" and said that if he could be of service to the President in reaching a workable agreement on the power question, "I am at your command." But after they had met again, Willkie wrote that he regretted seeing the battle between the Government and the utilities become "one of practically open warfare" and that the utilities "naturally feel they are fighting for their lives."

There was, as Willkie had said, "practically open warfare" as the TVA and the private companies raced to put up transmission lines so close together that in places they touched each other's poles. Here and there, fist fights broke out; there were meetings and demonstrations; and a Georgia woman took up a shotgun to hold off utility company pole-setters until the TVA men could get in. Willkie fought with additional court suits, with speeches, press statements, and a mammoth publicity campaign. He seemed to be in a dozen places at once, giving interviews, taking part in debates, and generally gaining favorable attention.

But President Roosevelt had made up his mind that the holding companies were at the root of the utility problem and that he intended to abolish them. He decided it was time to carry out his campaign promises for a drastic cleanup of the industry, and had the Public Utility Holding Company Act introduced into Congress while the TVA fight still went on. It was aimed directly at driving such companies as Commonwealth and Southern out of business.

Hearings on the holding company bill kept Congress and the public in an uproar for seven months. Willkie moved to Washington to lead the fight against it. He planned and managed the opposition strategy and appeared himself as a witness before House and Senate committees in explosive sessions that made top newspaper headlines. At his best in the witness chair, arguing with the skill and persuasion that had been his lifelong talent, Willkie challenged his Congressional inquisitors with questions of his own and as one reporter wrote: "neither gave nor asked any quarter." His quips brought laughter, and his proposals to correct the abuses of the holding companies without putting them out of existence won serious consideration.

Some Washington correspondents soon were likening Willkie to a David standing up before the Goliath of the Federal Government, "his rumpled hair and appearance making him look more a youthful college professor than a Wall Street magnate." Willkie did not sit at a table reading from a prepared statement, according to the *New York Herald Tribune*, "but strode up and down before the committee seated on a dais before him. At times his voice was angry as he turned to answer some allegation against holding companies, again it was soft . . ." Outside the hearings, he became a favorite with reporters, a colorful figure who made good news copy. He was a man who said things they could quote. Candid, openly friendly, and with a sense of the dramatic that created news, he gained many good friends among Washington newsmen and political columnists.

In and out of the committee hearings, he admitted Government regulation of holding companies was needed, and suggested specific laws for strict control that would end the writing up of stock values and the draining of funds from operating companies by the holding companies at the top. He threw open the records of his own corporation to show that it was well on the road toward correcting most of the abuses covered by the pending bill. Even Senator Burton K. Wheeler, one of the bill's sponsors and a stern critic of the utility industry, agreed that the record of Commonwealth and Southern under Willkie's management deserved praise. "I am frank to say to you," he told Willkie at the end of his testimony, "that probably if there had not been any more abuses in some companies than there have been in yours . . . you probably would not have been faced with some of the provisions that you are faced with at the present."

But the hearings also developed the sorry record of some of the other companies, with top-heavy financing that boosted rates for electricity and pyramids of control that sometimes towered thirteen companies high to let top stockholders benefit from millions of dollars in assets for comparatively small stock investments. At a press conference about holding companies, President Roosevelt simply asked, "Why have any?" And Will Rogers, in his newspaper column, wrote: "A holding company is a thing where you hand an accomplice the goods while the policeman searches you."

The real fight was over a section of the bill that set a limit of three years on the existence of all holding companies except those controlling "a single integrated system" of power production and distribution. It gave the Securities and Exchange Commission authority to decide which companies came under the rule. The section was known as the "Death Sentence" clause, a term Willkie invented himself to rally opposition against it.

Willkie lost his fight, but it was a close decision. Even with the full power of the Roosevelt administration behind it, the Death Sentence clause got through the Senate by the narrowest of margins, was first rejected by the House, and finally was squeezed into law in a compromise version of the bill by only a single vote. Willkie immediately announced a suit to test the new law, but he eventually lost that when the Supreme Court, two years later, upheld the Holding Company Act. He also lost all the suits against the TVA as the Supreme Court, over the years, handed down one decision after another in the Government's favor.

Forced to come to terms with the TVA, Willkie offered to sell his properties in the area to the Government for one hundred million dollars. The TVA offered fifty-five million. Willkie refused, and the off-and-on negotiations dragged along for four years. With each side fighting for a better bargaining position, the battle continued to rage in public while Willkie privately wrote the President, saw him at the White House, and had countless conferences with TVA Director Lilienthal.

Finally a compromise was reached, and Willkie got the Government to pay some seventy-eight million dollars, enough for Commonwealth and Southern to redeem all its outstanding bonds and securities and to realize about six million dollars for the holders of its common stock. A whole floor of New York's National City Bank was devoted to the three-hour ceremony of transferring checks and deeds, with speech-making on all sides, and flash bulbs popping as reporters crowded in for the story that was to put Willkie's name in banner headlines for his "one-man victory." As he held up a check made out for millions of dollars he said that for a country boy "it sure is a lot of money to be kicking around."

He emerged from the years of the Government power conflict a public figure, tested under the constant glare of publicity, skilled in the inner workings of Washington politics, practiced in winning public opinion, and a speaker who had broadened his themes from the utilities to the issues of Government itself. Articles he had written were appearing in big-circulation magazines; his husky voice was becoming familiar to radio audiences through interviews and debates; and his picture not only had been constantly in the newspapers but on the cover of a news magazine. His portrait had been painted; he was in the Social Register; and he numbered among his friends business leaders, congressmen, governors, writers, editors and publishers, and working newsmen in every state from Indiana to Mississippi as well as practically the entire corps of Washington correspondents. He had become a leading critic of the New Deal but also a champion of liberal causes, a Wall Street magnate who looked like a farmer and a Democrat who more often spoke like a Republican.

When Willkie returned to the University of Indiana on May 4, 1938, to deliver a Foundation Day address, he had been away from the campus for twenty-five years. He recalled the liberalism he had found there in his youth and spoke about what he had learned since about being a true liberal.

"Liberalism is not the property of any one political party nor the product of any one political platform," he said. "It is not a fixed program of action nor a vote on this or that particular measure. Liberalism is an attitude of mind. The criterion of the liberal philosophy is this: in the faith of the liberal the emphasis is upon individual freedom."

He went on to give what was perhaps the clearest definition of his philosophy he would ever make:

> The liberal movement strikes at the forces of autocracy whether they bear the label of business or government or society. . . . Perhaps I should warn you, however, that liberalism is neither easy nor sensational. Very rarely is it called upon to storm the barricades with flags waving, and very rarely can it rely simply upon a good heart to determine the merits of its cause. Frequently you will find yourself in the minority, and sometimes you will find yourself alone.
>
> The fact is that the liberal attempts to do the most difficult thing in the world—namely, to strike a true balance between the rights of the individual and the needs of society. He is like a man rowing a boat who when the boat swings to the right, pulls on the left, and when it swings to the left, pulls on the right. Liberalism sticks to the middle of the road, speaks quietly, and insists upon the color of no man's shirt.

Willkie publicly declared several times in 1938 that he was still a Democrat, and he voted for the full Democratic state ticket in New York to help reelect Governor Herbert H. Lehman over Republican Thomas E. Dewey, the young racket-busting district attorney. But as early as 1935, even while he was a member of the County Democratic Committee, he said that he wished he had back the money he had contributed to Franklin Roosevelt's first presidential campaign, and in 1936 he voted rather reluctantly for Republican Alf Landon, to avoid casting his ballot to continue the New Deal a second term.

Finally, in 1939, the conflict between his views and those of the majority of the party that had been his since his youth became too much of a contradiction for him to go on as a Democrat, and he became a Republican for the last five

105

years of his life. The decision had grown slowly and painfully, but the change itself was impulsive. On his way to register, his wife urged him to change his registration to Republican. He went inside without answering, but when he came out he said, "Well, I've done it." And afterwards he maintained, "I did not leave the Democratic party. The party left me."

Chapter Eleven

WENDELL WILLKIE was a rarity in American politics, a candidate for President whose nomination actually grew from popular demand. He made a reality of the myth that candidates are chosen by the people rather than by political bosses. The "Willkie boom" was well-directed, encouraged, and stage-managed by what some of those involved in it later boasted was "one of the best-engineered jobs" in the history of public relations, but the spark and fire came from Willkie himself, and they touched off a spontaneous explosion that rocketed him into the leadership of the Republican party.

The party bosses, the professional politicians without whom no man has a chance to be nominated or elected, were the last to accept Willkie. Many of them, especially the Old Guard conservatives long in party control, seemed to do so almost against their will. But the party was badly divided by factional groups, unable to find in its own ranks a leader who could bridge the gap between liberals and conservatives, and attract independent voters who for many different reasons had become disenchanted with the New Deal, so the

107

politicians at last gave in to the demand that, "We want Willkie!"

He set out in the beginning not to seek the Presidency but to win a hearing for the ideas in which he believed. With his voice, his pen, and his personality he stirred a groundswell of support so that many influential people, each as if he had made the discovery for himself, began to say, "There's a man who should be President." Long before anybody took the talk seriously, least of all Willkie himself, he began receiving hundreds of letters that offered to back him for the presidency. Encouraged by publicity, the suggestion grew.

Behind the publicity were editors, magazine publishers, journalists, writers, and other experts in the use of words. Some of them represented business and financial interests, liberal and reactionary, but most of them spread the word about Willkie because he was the sort of man they wanted to see in the White House. Among all his friends, those whose company he seemed to enjoy most were connected with the world of publishing. Despite his outward "country boy" manner, his main interests outside his work were literary. He was proud of book reviews he wrote, discussed writing a history of the pre-Civil War South, talked to publishers about other books he hoped to write, attended literary gatherings, invited poets and novelists to his home. One of his closest friends, upon whom he depended not only for literary help in preparing some of his manuscripts but also for advice in many of his career decisions, was Irita Van Doren, editor of the *New York Herald Tribune* book review section.

By 1939, he was writing for such varied publications as *The Saturday Evening Post, Forbes, Atlantic Monthly, Current History, Readers Digest, The New Republic,* and *Fortune.* He was a versatile enough writer to slant the style and content of his articles on national and international affairs so they would appeal to each group of readers. Sometimes he would have completely different articles on the same basic theme in two or more magazines in the same month. As his fame grew, so did the demand for his writing, and there was such a response to some of his articles that magazines reprinted them for distribution in pamphlet form.

While he was writing for the magazines, they were writing about him. *The Saturday Evening Post* told of his utility industry battles with the Government as *The Man Who Talked Back*. He was featured in a *Time* cover story, praised for his ability as a corporation executive in articles in *Fortune* and *Life*. A filmed documentary pictured his Washington activities, newsreels showed his congressional appearances and visits to the White House, and radio programs as well as accounts in newspaper magazine sections were devoted to his articulate pleas for an end to the conflict between business and government.

But even more than what he wrote and what was written about him, his speeches up and down the country inspired an enthusiastic following. They were well-reported in the press and often broadcast by radio, but their greatest effect was upon those who heard him in person. He was a man charged with vitality, with urgency, with a seeming ability to put into simple and direct words what many of his listeners wished they could say. Many seemed to find in him the sense of identification they felt watching the bold hero on a movie screen, the man who dared to speak up and was afraid of nobody, twice as big as life and yet "just an ordinary guy." He had something to say, and said it logically and to the point.

He talked about the rights of the individual and the needs of society, the effect upon the nation of the quarrels which had caused "class warfare" between the New Deal and the business community, the "grim and inescapable fact" that after six New Deal years "we have as many people unemployed as at the beginning." It was time, he said, to take another look at the spread of government controls, not only in terms of the evils they certainly had helped to correct but with a view toward what would now encourage initiative and productivity, because "while a straitjacket will keep a man out of trouble it is not a suitable garment in which to work."

A favorite theme of Willkie's was that the evils of big government were threatening to become as overpowering as the evils of big business had been in his youth and that individual liberty should be protected against the sins and excesses of both. More and more, he vigorously defended civil liberties. Demanding the preservation of free speech, he lashed out at courts that punished Communists or even pro-Nazis for "political opinion" more than for their alleged crimes. At a time when it was considered "radical" to voice any criticism of the House Committee on Un-American Activities, Willkie thoroughly denounced the Committee's methods. "Let me say to you," he warned in a speech to Columbia University alumni, "that the democratic process cannot go on, and will be gradually undermined, if men can be put on the witness stand without protection of counsel and without any adequate opportunity to answer. There is no more cruel way of destroying the reputation of a man than by publicity through inference and innuendo. This must be stopped."

Speaking of his own experience as a witness before other committees of Congress, he jokingly said that his private papers, telegrams and bank accounts had been examined so many times that he was reluctant to sign wires to his own wife with the word "Love" for fear of what some congressional snoopers might try to make of them.

Two million listeners had a chance to hear him at his best in a debate with Robert H. Jackson, then Assistant Attorney

110

General and later a Supreme Court Justice, on radio's most popular public affairs program, *Town Meeting of the Air,* on January 6, 1938. The debate, over what was needed to restore cooperation between business and government, was one of the liveliest of the series, broken by outbursts of applause as well as by boos and outcries from the studio audience. Again, in a less serious role, he was guest star of the enormously popular *Information Please* program, then the nation's favorite quiz show. Such appearances, plus the mounting newspaper and magazine publicity, brought him hundreds of requests to speak at all sorts of public affairs. At one point, he had received a total of more than two thousand invitations to address various groups, and they kept coming in such numbers it took the full time of a secretary just to turn down those he couldn't accept.

The one issue upon which he stood almost alone among possible contenders for the Republican nomination was that of world cooperation. Despite the rise of fascism in Europe, many Americans were not deeply concerned about foreign policy in the spring of 1938 when Willkie was saying: "Today the institutions of democracy and individual liberty are under question. Mussolini, Hitler and Stalin believe the democratic form of government is obsolete. The surrender of liberalism to the theory of the totalitarian state would mean the sacrifice of free man's achievement."

But within two years, Europe's cold war had become hot, and the frightening reality of Nazi military might brought a change in American opinion. While many Americans were still isolationist, an increasing number favored aid to the European democracies. Other leading candidates for the Republican nomination were slow to admit there was any grave threat to America in what was happening in Europe, but Willkie firmly declared that "today the world is so closely knit, the oceans are so small, and the peoples of the

111

world are so dependent upon each other, that it is not realistic to make domestic policies without considering their relationship to foreign affairs." He said, "It makes a great deal of difference to us—politically, economically, emotionally—what kind of a world exists beyond our shores."

The first important newspaper columnist to connect Willkie's name with the 1940 presidential nominations was Arthur Krock of *The New York Times*. On February 23, 1939, Krock devoted his editorial page column to the talk that was going on in Washington about possible Republican nominees. After listing "odds-on favorites," he quoted capital gossip to the effect that "you can't wholly count out Willkie, but he'll have to go down as the darkest horse in the stable."

A few weeks later, *Newsweek*'s Raymond Moley commented on the fact that "a few timid feelers" were being put out about Willkie as a possible candidate. Other columnists began to mention the dim chance of his nomination and by midsummer 1939, *Time* magazine, describing Willkie as a "lifelong Indiana Democrat" and "the only business man in the U.S. who is ever mentioned as a presidential possibility for 1940," said that he was receiving hundreds of letters a week urging him "to keep up the fight, many predicting that it will wind up with him in the White House."

The "Willkie boom" grew louder in November when General Hugh S. Johnson, one-time head of the National Recovery Administration, who had parted with the New Deal and become its caustic critic, suggested in a speech in New York, and later in his syndicated column, that "if Mr. Willkie were nominated, he would make a powerful candidate, and if elected, a great president." Willkie, who was in Atlanta on a business trip, joked about it with reporters who reached him there. "In view of the speed with which the government is taking over my business, I'll soon have to be looking around for a new job," he said. "General Johnson's is the best offer I've had so far."

Coming as it did after all the publicity that had gone before, the exchange of comments made headlines that focused national attention upon Willkie as a possible candidate. It posed the definite question and the results were explosive. What had been a comparative trickle of letters, messages, and telegrams became a flood. Thousands of people from all over the country began urging him to seek the nomination.

But as the election year of 1940 began, Willkie hadn't made up his mind. He went on making several speeches a week, testing public reaction to his ideas, but said, "I'm not running for President" and that the nomination "of course, is not going to happen." Yet he kept speculation alive by adding that however unlikely such a possibility seemed, "if the nomination were given me without any strings, I would have to accept it" because "no man in middle life and good health could do otherwise. But I couldn't go out and seek delegates and make two-sided statements. I value my independence. That's what I've been fighting for all these years."

His mother died in Elwood on March 10, 1940, at the age of eighty-two, shortly after she had written him, following one of his radio appearances, "to tell you how proud I am of you and of your standing in this great nation." She had carried on the family law practice for a while after Willkie's father died, then had lived for a time in Maryland, and finally had returned to Elwood to make her home with a relative and to take an interest in the public library she helped establish. She suffered a heart attack on a Saturday evening and died the next day. The epitaph Willkie and his brothers chose for her gravestone was: "She was driven by an indomitable will." He confided to his brothers, after the

113

funeral, that he was seriously considering making a fight to win the presidential nomination, but that he still wasn't entirely convinced he had a chance.

He put himself more firmly on record in support of aid to the European democracies, even though such views went against the strong isolationism of Old Guard Republicans, and *The New York Times* commented that he was saying things "supposed to be fatal to anyone hoping for the Republican nomination." At a meeting of the American Newspaper Publishers' Association, he called for "helping the democracies in every way possible within the limits of international law" and warned that "if the totalitarian states prevail the odds are very substantial that we shall have to meet them in armed conflict when they have been victorious over the democracies and are truculent and strong."

It was on April 9, 1940, that Nazi Germany invaded Denmark and Norway and started its crushing military advance across Europe, and the events of history began to turn American opinion strongly in Willkie's favor. Finally jolted into taking a new look at the world and America's relations to it, many people also took a new look at him and listened to what he was saying.

That same month, *Fortune* magazine, edited by Russell Davenport, who soon was to resign to devote his full time to managing Willkie's campaign, published an article by Willkie, called *We, the People, A Foundation for a Political Platform for Recovery*. It was a ringing declaration of his faith in free enterprise, followed by a summation of his views in the form of a petition that those who agreed with him might want to endorse as a declaration to party leaders "before the political platforms are written." Widely circulated in pamphlet form, it started various bankers, industrialists, advertising agency executives, public relations experts, and even some politicians, planning separately and

Wendell Willkie as a naval cadet at the Culver Military Academy in 1906, Culver, Indiana.

Wendell Willkie as a lawyer in Akron, Ohio, at age of 37.

Willkie as a member of the 325th Field Artillery in France during World War I.

Willkie, as President of Commonwealth and Southern, leaving White House, November 23, 1937 after conference with President Roosevelt.

ABOVE: Willkie as Republican Presidential nominee in Rushville, Ind. Left to right: Miss Sleeth, Mrs. Cora Wilk, the mother of Mrs. Willkie, and Mrs. Willkie. July 17, 1940.

RIGHT: Willkie, as Republican Presidential Nominee, acknowledging cheers of Convention, July 22, 1940.

Willkie, as Republican candidate for President, with his wife and son, Philip. August 1, 1940.

Acme Photo

Wendell Willkie chats with Mayor Fiorello H. LaGuardia and Mrs. J. Borden Harriman at a rally of Committee to Defend America by Aiding the Allies. May 7, 1941.

Acme Photo

Wendell Willkie, left, and Winston Churchill emerge from
10 Downing Street, London. February 5, 1941.

together what specific steps they could take to support the movement to win Willkie the Republican nomination.

First to translate the boom into the active support of thousands of voters was an amateur at politics, Oren Root, Jr., a twenty-nine-year-old lawyer and grandnephew of one-time Republican Secretary of State, Elihu Root. He had never met Willkie, although he had heard him speak at Princeton and had been impressed, but when he read *We, the People,* he decided Willkie was his own choice for president. To learn how many others felt the same way, Root spent forty dollars to print and mail "a couple of thousand" simple declarations, each with space for fifteen signatures of those who might favor Willkie's candidacy. Willkie knew nothing about it until Root dropped him a note, explaining what he had done just as "a feeler and a very small beginning."

Within five days Root had to print twenty thousand more, and from the day his first declarations were sent out, his phone "never stopped ringing" with eager offers of support. Hundreds of people who signed the originals began to send out copies made at their own expense and those, in turn, were copied and circulated by others. A small classified advertisement in the Public Notices column of a New York newspaper, asking for contributions to spread the movement, started bringing in money at the rate of two hundred dollars a day.

Root took a leave of absence from his law firm, rented an empty store, and set up the first full-time Willkie Club headquarters. He used the small contributions to put classified ads in other papers across the country, urging the establishment of local Willkie Clubs. In a month there were five hundred Willkie Clubs, and new ones were forming at the rate of twenty a day as people volunteered their services, time, and money. Eventually there were at least fifty thousand Willkie volunteers in the field, handing out buttons, distributing campaign kits and Willkie literature, and collecting more than three million signatures to petitions.

Other volunteer groups were formed. Prominent people began voicing their endorsement. The editors and publicists went to work to quicken the public pulse. Here and there, a Republican leader announced that he was backing Willkie. By May, a public opinion poll of candidates preferred by Republican voters included his name, still a poor fourth on a list that gave him only three per cent against sixty-seven per cent for Thomas E. Dewey. But at least Willkie was among those mentioned. When his son Philip was chosen by Princeton classmates as the member of the senior class who was "most likely to succeed," *The New York Times* commented editorially that it was "a question a good many people are now asking about the young man's father."

Six weeks before the nominating convention, Willkie was still not a declared candidate and had not made up his mind whether to stage an all-out fight for the nomination. "I'm not electioneering," he insisted, but only "trying to win popular support for certain principles in which I believe." That support had grown swiftly, but he had yet to convince the party's professional politicians. Among the publishers who had become his friends were John and Gardner Cowles, Jr., who owned *Look* magazine, and newspapers in Minnesota and Iowa. In a conference with Willkie and Russell Davenport, the Cowleses suggested that he should make a test of his appeal to the politicians themselves, the men who would really decide the nomination.

Willkie reluctantly agreed that he "didn't have anything to lose," and arrangements were made for him to speak at a meeting of Minnesota Republicans who were planning to gather in St. Paul on May 11. Harold Stassen, the state's popular young Republican governor, was asked to introduce Willkie at the meeting. On his way to Minnesota, Willkie stopped off in Chicago to see his brother Ed, and told him that he had decided he would go on with the campaign if the speech were a success. But he indicated that if it failed, he might as well forget the possibility of becoming president and get back to work untangling the affairs of the Commonwealth and Southern Corporation.

The St. Paul speech was almost a failure. Anxious to impress the seven hundred Republicans at the meeting, as well as a listening radio audience, Willkie had agreed to read a carefully-prepared text, and the result was so dull there was only polite applause as he heard the announcer say, "And now we return you to the studio." Willkie crushed the pages in his hands, hurled the ball of paper into the air, faced the group, and said, "Some damned fool convinced me I had to read a speech to you. Now let me tell you what I really think!"

He launched into an inspired extemporaneous talk that lasted twenty minutes, changed the whole impression he had made, and brought the politicians to their feet to cheer him for a full ten minutes after he had finished. Before he had left the hall, ten of the Minnesota delegates personally gave him their pledge that they would vote for him at the Philadelphia convention.

Willkie said that was the night when he first became convinced that he had a chance to win. When he returned to New York, he issued an announcement asking everyone working on his behalf to get in touch with Russell Davenport to plan an organized campaign. From then on, he gave it every minute of his time, fighting to get the nomination. He had a series of conferences with various party leaders, and during the remaining weeks before the convention made frankly

117

political speeches to Republican audiences in fourteen cities in Iowa, New Jersey, New York, Kansas, Ohio, Colorado, Missouri, Nebraska, and three New England states.

"Let us work together. We have had enough of discord," was his theme. "Let us bring together the industrial brains of this country, and the labor of this country, and let us take our vast resources out of the earth and transport them to our factories; and let us assign each factory a job for the defense of this nation. Let us gear these jobs, one to the other, so that each will fit, so there will be a minimum of waste, and so that our army, our navy, and our air force may be adequately equipped as quickly as possible." And he said, "I should like to ask Secretary Hull to ask the democracies, publicly and openly in the name of the American people, what help—short of troops—the American people can give."

Chapter Twelve

WENDELL WILLKIE, in a rush as usual, hopped aboard a train in New York's Pennsylvania Station to head for the Republican National Convention in Philadelphia and discovered that in his hurry he had left his money at home, so reporters chipped in to buy his ticket. He talked the whole distance, cocked his flat-brimmed straw hat on his head, and stepped out onto the Philadelphia platform to be greeted by cheers that hardly stopped until the convention was over.

He arrived on Saturday, June 22, 1940, two days before the convention was to open, and set up his headquarters in a modest two-room hotel suite, a fact the newspapers made much of, since Senator Robert Taft's organization had 102 rooms, and Thomas E. Dewey's had 78. From the time Willkie moved in, delegates who wanted to meet him were lined up all the way along the hall to the elevators. Within twenty-four hours Willkie had shaken hands with an estimated six hundred delegates or alternates, searching out those who didn't come to see him, and before the convention got down to voting, he had talked to all or part of the dele-

119

gations from thirty-four states. Sprawled in a chair, or seated on the floor as they circled him, he answered all questions fired at him with what reporters called "astounding frankness."

The Willkie Clubs had recruited five hundred volunteer "young salesmen" to buttonhole arriving delegates and sell them on Willkie, and also had inspired followers in cities across the country to send large groups of "plain American citizens" to Philadelphia to support Willkie's candidacy. They and hundreds of others who swarmed into the city until hotels were overflowing soon had all of Philadelphia in a whirlwind of pro-Willkie activities, demonstrations, songfests, and parades. Willkie buttons sprouted on coat lapels; automobiles spilled out bands of appropriately straw-hatted Willkie enthusiasts; and delegates' hotel rooms, dining tables, and coat pockets became inundated with Willkie pamphlets. Some delegates found Willkie handbills folded into their newspapers, wrapped in shirts that came back from the laundry, suits returned from the cleaner, and even tucked under their pillows by hotel maids.

Other Willkie volunteers, working in the delegates' home areas over the nation, started telephones ringing with long-distance calls from influential local citizens who kept up a steady barrage of personal appeals for his nomination. They sent telegrams, letters, postcards by the thousands. One delegate alone said that he found three thousand pro-Willkie messages awaiting him when he checked into his hotel. Before the convention opened, it was estimated that delegates were sent well over one million Willkie telegrams and letters from the voters back home, and they increased as the convention went on. There were charges that the huge mailing campaign was rigged and that some of the letters bore identical wording. But while it was planned and carried out at the urging of Willkie workers, there was never proof that the signatures were less than genuine. The Willkie demonstrations, in and out of the convention hall, also were encouraged if not stage-managed by Willkie workers, but they grew from the genuine enthusiasm of supporters.

"I would like to think it means I'm quite a fellow," Willkie said about the public response, "but I think it means I represent a trend—or am ahead of a trend." He felt the nation was trending toward the sort of liberalism he advocated and that the Republican party would have to become less conservative if it wanted to win the people's votes. Declaring his independence from the old-line party bosses, he had said, "I am one hundred per cent against . . . turning the Republican party back to the days of Harding and Coolidge." But there was also a greater trend he was leading, perhaps the one that did more than anything else to win him the nomination, and that was the swing of American public opinion away from the isolationists who dominated the party.

By the time the convention opened in Philadelphia, the whole of Western civilization seemed threatened by the sweep of Hitler's military power. France had fallen and lay prostrate. Norway, Denmark, Luxembourg, the Netherlands, and Belgium had been overrun, enslaved or left in ruin. England stood alone and seemingly defenseless after Dunkirk, separated by only twenty miles of water from the final crush of Nazi might. America was in an uproar over what to do, how far to go in aiding Britain, if aid were to be given at all. There were those like Willkie who insisted that only by helping the Allies could democracy be saved from destruction and America itself saved from eventual attack. Others feared that America was being "dragged into war to save England." On both sides there were all degrees of opinion that had produced a fury of debate, and the political conventions came in the midst of it.

121

But the great majority of Americans, both Republicans and Democrats favored aid to Britain, and among leading contenders for the Republican nomination Willkie alone symbolized that national feeling. Senator Robert Taft was strongly isolationist, Michigan's Arthur Vandenberg hadn't yet come to change his mind on the issue, and Thomas E. Dewey's position was unclear since he had made speeches on both sides of the question. Most of the Old Guard party bosses, especially Republican leaders in Congress, were isolationist. But many convention delegates felt they had to heed the trend of public opinion toward aid to the Allies if they hoped to put forward a candidate who had any chance of winning the election.

Dewey, New York's thirty-eight-year-old district attorney, was the overwhelming choice for the nomination, according to all the polls when the convention opened. Taft had solid support among the conservatives and his delegate strength was well organized. He was predicting victory after the first ballot. Vandenberg's backers counted on a convention deadlock. Willkie's own prediction was that while he would trail at the beginning, he would capture the nomination "on the sixth or seventh ballot."

He had come to the convention without much of a political organization behind him, but he gathered a working team of senators, governors and others prominent in the party. National Republican Chairman John Hamilton, while he had to remain neutral, was sympathetic to Willkie's candidacy. Harold Stassen, the convention's keynote speaker, announced his support of Willkie and became his floor manager. Willkie's opponents tried to launch a "Stop Willkie" movement, but failed to pull it together. Ironically, the anti-Willkie forces included Senate Republican leader Charles McNary of Oregon, later to become his running mate, who predicted at the convention's start that the Willkie boom would quickly collapse.

When the delegates got down to the real business of nominating a candidate late Wednesday afternoon, the huge and hot convention hall was jammed with 22,000 people, and it was estimated that two-thirds of those who packed the galleries as visitors were for Willkie. The nominating speech for Dewey stressed the fact that, unlike Willkie, he was a "lifelong Republican," and the parading demonstration that followed lasted twenty-five minutes—the longest of the convention. The nineteen-minute demonstration for Taft seemed even more intense. Again, in the nomination speech for Taft, there was an indirect slap at Willkie as a Republican-come-lately, rather than an Old Guard stalwart. Taft, the delegates were told, was "not the best backslapper, but has the best backbone."

Eight states passed their turns in the roll call to give the microphone to Congressman Charles Halleck of Indiana, and from that moment the galleries went wild as the "Willkie amateurs" all but took over the convention. It is standing tradition that a candidate's name is never mentioned until the end of a nominating speech, but Halleck broke the tradition by naming Willkie at the start, and the waiting galleries broke into a tremendous roar and began to chant, "We want Willkie!" The chant punctuated every sentence of Halleck's speech.

Halleck spoke of the man who "without a political organization and no campaign fund" had become "the hope of people in every walk of life and in every corner of the land." True, he said, it was only recently that Willkie had joined the Republicans, but he asked, "Is the Republican party a closed corporation? Do you have to be born in it?" The galleries answered with a ringing shout of, "No! We want

Willkie!" By then some of the delegates were booing back at the galleryites, but the chanting only grew louder. "There is a man big enough to be President of the United States," Halleck finished. "Wendell Lewis Willkie."

The cheering was as if "all of Niagara Falls roared over into Convention Hall." Down on the floor, Willkie's friends among the delegates wrested the New York standard from the hands of angry Dewey men and started a wild disorganized parade in which other delegates joined. Fights and scuffles broke out as the standards of more states were seized by the Willkie marchers, and the galleries settled into the constant chanting: "We want Willkie!" Chairman Joseph Martin futilely banged his gavel to restore order. He appealed to the crowd: "The chair must remind the occupants of the galleries that they are the guests of the convention." Above the din, a shout came back, "Guests, nothing! We *are* the convention!"

Outside the hall, other Willkie demonstrators who had been unable to get into the galleries took up the chant as they paraded through the streets. Inside, it took twenty minutes of gavel-pounding to produce enough quiet for Willkie's seconding speeches to be heard, and then the convention recessed until morning. But the uproar continued, and delegates returning to their hotel rooms made their way through streets filled with shouting Willkie supporters. When they reached their hotels there were still more Willkie letters, telegrams, bundles of petitions, and personal messages from people in their home districts awaiting them. Some delegates were resentful and thoroughly sick of being badgered to vote for Willkie, yet they were also impressed.

After more nominations the next day, the balloting began late in the afternoon. Willkie's first two votes came from

Arkansas and touched off a roar from the crowded galleries, which soon again became the familiar chant, "We want Willkie!" Delegates protested that the hall was so noisy they couldn't hear what was going on. Chairman Martin called the sergeants-at-arms to clear the aisles of unauthorized campaigners who had invaded the floor itself for a last minute buttonholing of delegates. But the galleryites kept up their incessant beating chant most of the night.

Dewey, as expected, easily took the lead on the first ballot with 360 votes. Taft was second with 189, and Willkie collected 105 from twenty-four states, with the rest of the one thousand votes scattered among ten other candidates. Waiting out the ordeal in his hotel room with a small group of reporters, Willkie listened to the returns by radio and also had a direct phone line to Harold Stassen on the convention floor. As he followed the balloting, Willkie kept up a running commentary, joking with the reporters. He paced the room at times, smoked his way through packs of cigarettes, drank quarts of coffee.

On the second ballot, Dewey lost some of his lead, Taft gained, and Willkie also picked up additional votes. The convention was recessed for dinner, and in his room, Willkie took time out for a steak and a bowl of raspberries. By the time the third ballot was taken, after the dinner recess, Willkie had moved into second place behind Dewey, and he went into the lead for the first time on the fourth ballot. Dewey clearly was out of the race, but he was still holding one-fourth of the votes, and Taft had begun a rapid climb and expected to pick up most of Dewey's votes along with others.

Taft men were predicting that it was "in the bag" for their candidate, and a few reporters were so certain of it they began sending out premature stories that Taft had been

125

nominated. Even Willkie's composure was shaken, and he admitted to the reporters in his room: "Well, Taft might get it—but at least I scared them."

The battle became so intense that Taft and Willkie each gained exactly the same number of votes on the fifth ballot, but Willkie's lead put him only seventy-two votes short of the nomination. Previous Republican conventions had gone beyond a fifth ballot only four times in history. Taft forces tried for a recess to hold the voting over until the next day, but their move came too late, and a sixth ballot began. Both sides held doggedly until Senator Vandenberg released Michigan's delegation, and 35 votes swung to Willkie. Oklahoma and Oregon widened the crack, and finally Virginia gave him one more vote than the total needed. Then one state after another switched to board the bandwagon. The motion was made unanimous, and Wendell Willkie became the Republican candidate for President. It was, as he had predicted, the sixth ballot that brought victory.

Reporters rushed to his hotel to join the small group that had been with him, and some expected Willkie to be ready with his usual jokes and wisecracks. Instead he quietly said, "I'm very happy, very humble, and very proud." It was then two o'clock in the morning, the balloting had gone on all night, and he was a very tired man who excused himself to join his family.

A vice-presidential candidate still had to be chosen, and traditionally the choice was up to Willkie, but when party leaders suggested Oregon's Senator McNary in a move to unite Republican factions, Willkie agreed. He held no grudge against McNary for his part in the "Stop Willkie" movement. McNary first refused and flatly declared, "I wouldn't run with Willkie." But former presidential candidate, Alf Landon, and others urged him and he finally accepted "for the good of the party."

So, the following day, the convention nominated isolationist McNary, a strong supporter of public electric power and New Deal social security and labor programs, to be the running mate of interventionist, New Deal critic, and private utility magnate Willkie. If they made strange political bedfellows, they also offered proof of Willkie's hope that he somehow could unite a party that was badly divided.

Soaked by rain that failed to dampen the enthusiasm of thousands who lined the Philadelphia streets, his hair sprinkled with the confetti they had showered over him, Willkie went to Convention Hall to thank the delegates before they adjourned. With his wife beside him, he stood on the platform in the spotlights, waved to the wildly cheering throng, and stepped to the cluster of microphones that would carry his voice to the world.

"I stand before you without a single pledge, promise or understanding of any kind except for the advancement of your cause and the preservation of American democracy," he said. "Democracy, and our way of life, is facing the most crucial test it has ever faced in all its long history; and we are here not as Republicans alone but as Americans, to dedicate ourselves to the democratic way of life in the United States because here stands the last firm, untouched foothold of freedom in all the world. We all have the common purpose at this time that this way of life shall not pass from the earth."

And then the man who nearly all his life had been a Democrat made it deliberately clear that he meant to appeal to the people of all parties and not merely to those who had nominated him. "And so, you Republicans," he said, "I call upon you to join me, help me." He waved once more to the crowd, grinned, and said, "I think I'll go home now and sleep for a week."

Chapter Thirteen

W^{ENDELL} WILLKIE enjoyed a few days' rest, cruising slowly back to New York from Philadelphia aboard publisher Roy Howard's yacht, but it was the last rest he had until the campaign was over. His first day in New York, he held two press conferences, resigned as head of Commonwealth and Southern Corporation and wound up his business affairs, lunched with Harold Stassen, conferred with Thomas Dewey, roughly outlined his campaign schedule, and that night went to Radio City Music Hall to see himself as an actor in a filmed version of the *Information Please* program, where he was recognized in the audience and greeted with a show-stopping chant of "We want Willkie!"

He flew to Washington a few days later to confer with his running mate, Senator McNary, removed John Hamilton as National Committee Chairman, and persuaded the party's congressional leader, Joseph W. Martin, to take on that added task, and tried to merge his personal forces with the party machine in a way that would give each group separate power. Russell Davenport remained his personal manager, and Oren Root was in charge of the Willkie Clubs and other volunteers. Hamilton became Executive Director, leader of the professional politicians and in charge of campaign tactics, and Martin became chief planner of strategy. But the setup never worked out too well because the party professionals and Willkie amateurs were in conflict throughout the campaign.

At the end of the week, on July 9, 1940, he took off for what was announced as a three-week vacation in Colorado Springs, accompanied by his family, his secretary, a dozen reporters, and four photographers. It was a "vacation" Willkie later called "the most strenuous in my life" and his Eastern campaign manager, Samuel Pryor, said that "all the 'screwballs' in the United States visited him while he was out there" and left him "mentally fatigued before the campaign started."

Willkie was besieged by all the people with whom an ambitious candidate must shake hands and pose for the camera, as well as by state officials, minor party candidates, congressmen, publishers, businessmen, Republican leaders, and disgruntled Democrats. He lunched with former President Hoover and former presidential candidate Alf Landon. There were statements to make on every subject that came up in the news, quick plane flights to party conferences, visits to rodeos, the sugar-beet fields, Founders' Day programs, and other civic affairs. Among typical publicity jaunts was a drive 182 miles across the Continental Divide with Mrs. Willkie, so he could voice his approval of the scenic splendors of the West and visit the four-house hamlet of Almont, where a crowd of seven thousand had gathered for "an old fashioned fish fry." Serenaded by a thirty-piece band, Willkie ate four trout, pronounced them wonderful, and delivered a brief speech about the preservation of American democracy.

Left without enough time to work out his thoughts on

129

campaign policy, trying to plan the campaign itself and work on his acceptance speech, he was mentally and physically nearly exhausted. All the while he was doing his best to preserve not only outward party harmony, but to hold the working support of conservatives and old-line party bosses, some of whom he felt refused to face the fact that he had to appeal to millions of voters outside the party because there simply weren't enough Republicans to win the election. He insisted upon making a strong and liberal personal crusade; they insisted his first duty was to unify the party.

The differences went deeper than party organization. Many Republicans wanted him to condemn the Democrats, Roosevelt, and the whole of the New Deal in blistering, hard-hitting, uncompromising attacks. Willkie instead openly admitted that the New Deal had accomplished many needed reforms. In international affairs, he practically ignored the party platform and approved most of the goals if not the methods of the Roosevelt foreign policy. In the beginning, he tried to compromise, to accept for the sake of party harmony some views he did not thoroughly endorse, and even at times to make the sort of all-out anti-New Deal attacks the party bosses wanted to hear, but on basic principles he refused to budge. By the time the campaign was over, he felt he had gone too far in trying to compromise with party conservatives.

Meanwhile, the Democratic National Convention in Chicago had renominated President Roosevelt; and Willkie, listening to the proceedings by radio in Colorado Springs, said, "I'm deeply gratified at the chance to meet the champ. It ought to be a great campaign." He looked forward to debating the issues of the New Deal with "the author and ablest advocate of that philosophy."

But President Roosevelt made it clear in his acceptance

130

speech that his strategy would be to ignore the entire Willkie campaign as much as possible, keep himself aloof from direct debates and the heat of campaign battles, and let his lieutenants do the active campaigning for him. "I shall not have the time nor inclination to indulge in purely political debate," he declared. To which Willkie answered: "I predict that Mr. Roosevelt will be out on the stump before this election is over."

In the same speech, the President launched his own campaign by shrewdly stressing the isolationist sympathies of many Republicans and planting the question in the public mind as to whether Willkie had the experience to manage the government in a time of growing world emergency. Roosevelt set the theme other Democrats would follow until election day, and raised the doubt that probably more than any other caused Willkie's defeat when he said: "If our government should pass into other hands next January, untried hands, inexperienced hands, we can only hope and pray that they will not substitute appeasement and compromise with those who would destroy democracy everywhere, including here."

Willkie left Colorado Springs in mid-August for Rushville, where he and his wife were joined by Philip, who had been on an automobile vacation trip. He enjoyed seeing his farms, boasting genially about Indiana hogs, and strolling around his wife's home town to point out to reporters the house where he had first met her. Not far away in his own home town of Elwood, frantic preparations were underway for the biggest outdoor carnival that part of Indiana had ever seen. It hadn't been planned that way when arrangements first were made for him to deliver his acceptance speech from the steps of the Elwood High School to an expected crowd of a few thousand. But a quarter of a million people had begun

131

pouring into Elwood, aboard special trains, buses, motorcades, and in automobiles that choked highways in all directions.

The high school site had been abandoned for forty-acre Calloway Park, with 160 acres of farm land around it cleared of crops for parking space. The speaker's stand alone would hold one thousand honored guests, and every folding chair in the county had been rounded up to provide rows of seats for thirty thousand more, but the other tens of thousands would stand. First-aid tents, rest rooms, a few hundred drinking fountains, and thirty large tents to accommodate press, radio, and political groups were set up. Railroads built special platforms, new telephone and telegraph cables were laid, and nearly one thousand police were put on special duty. Hot dog and hamburger stands and Willkie souvenir booths sprang up by the dozens, and champion flagpole-sitter Shipwreck Kelly mounted a nearby flagpole to advertise coffee. As the crowd moved in on the little town of ten thousand where Willkie had been born and raised, all the carnival lacked was its star performer.

By the time Willkie arrived at noon on August 17, the temperature had risen to 102° in the shade, the restless crowds were as drenched with sweat as he was, and were heat-weary and impatient for him to deliver the verbal fireworks they expected. But they had three hours more to wait in the sun as he rode around Elwood, standing in an open touring car and waving his straw hat, his procession halted everywhere by tangled traffic and surging humanity. He managed to say a few words from the high school steps, to greet old classmates and townsfolk, and finally, at three in the afternoon, reached the speaker's stand. While the crowd munched food, swilled soft drinks, pushed, shoved, goggled, and chased stray children, Willkie began a discussion of "the political philosophy that is in my heart."

He charged that the New Deal sought safety instead of risk, distribution of what people already had instead of the production of more, acceptance instead of discovery, that it destroyed the incentive to invention and took the spirit from free adventure. The New Deal, having been dealt, he said, "has refused to make any more bets on the American future." Free to admit that he approved many of the New Deal's farm policies, business, banking and labor reforms, collective bargaining, wage and hour standards, federal pensions, old age benefits and unemployment insurance, Willkie nevertheless attacked its "doctrine of division" rather than growth. By its maze of controls and restraints, taxation and spending, and by provoking class hatreds between capital and labor, business and government, he said it limited production and freedom.

But he refused to take the stand that many Republican leaders had urged him to take against the Selective Service Act which had been introduced into Congress. He was warned that unless he opposed it, he would lose the votes of thousands of Americans who were strongly against a peacetime draft of young men. Instead, Willkie courageously came out for it in his acceptance speech. He declared: "I cannot ask the American people to put their faith in me without realizing my conviction that some form of selective service is the only democratic way to secure the trained and competent manpower we need for national defense." His refusal to make a campaign issue of selective service helped the backers of it put the draft through Congress and into operation to build the nation's armed strength.

He also refused to duck the flaming controversy over aid to Britain, which party leaders had advised him to keep quiet about or to soft-pedal in his acceptance speech. As he spoke, Nazi bombers had begun to lay the cities of England in ruin, and he told the listening crowd that "we know that we are not isolated from those suffering people" and that "we cannot brush the pitiless picture of their destruction from our vision or escape the profound effects of it upon the world in which we live." Directly answering the isolationists who were powerful in his own party, he said the time had come for America to honestly face its relationship with Britain and admit that its defeat "would be calamity for us." He faced it by pledging his "wholehearted support" to President Roosevelt "in whatever action he may take" to extend to Britain the material resources of the United States.

But the crowd in Elwood had gathered to see a circus, and Willkie was neither clown nor lion tamer. He had tried to define a philosophy of government, and to show exactly where his kind of liberalism differed from that of the New Deal. He had tried to explain the personal convictions upon which he would campaign. It was a speech that read well in print, but Willkie was never at his best when he tried to read a prepared address. It was the wrong speech for that day and that crowd, and after the tremendous buildup, it fell flat with a dull thud heard across the country. The speech that was supposed to skyrocket his campaign had sputtered out in a fizzle.

There was automatic applause from the yelling throngs as he left the carnival town that had been his home, and afterwards some scattered praise in the newspapers. But, to many, it sounded too much as though he had said that he approved most of the New Deal but wanted a chance to show he could run it better than President Roosevelt had. As one critic put it: "He agreed with Mr. Roosevelt's entire program of social reform and said it was leading to disaster."

Secretary of the Interior Harold Ickes, chosen by President Roosevelt to answer Willkie's acceptance speech, sarcastically called him a "simple, barefoot Wall Street lawyer"

134

who was trying to pose as "the rich man's Roosevelt" and win votes by endorsing reform legislation he had once opposed. He accused Willkie of "fleeing to Indiana" to escape the "stigma" of his banking and political associations in New York.

With the Elwood acceptance carnival over, the Willkie managers went on to stage another show in Rushville, where Willkie established his political base. It was a continuous performance in which he was cast by publicity men in the starring role of a small-town Indiana farmer "forgetting politics for a time" as he lolled in a rural setting that would present him to America as the homespun country boy the publicists tried to make of him. To Willkie's credit, he himself insisted, "There is one error I want to correct—this talk of being a Rush County farmer. I am purely a conversational farmer. I have never done a stroke of work on a Rush County farm in my life and I hope I never have to." He also stubbornly refused to pose for photographers while wearing overalls or sitting on a tractor. But pictures were taken of him in barnyard settings, and his publicity men capitalized on his genuine love of his farms and the Indiana town.

At a time when a good part of the world was aflame and the nation was concerned with the vital decisions being forced upon it by the war in Europe, the "farm boy image" struck a false note with many Americans. Willkie's farm manager, Mary Sleeth, commented, "It's getting so every time a cameraman shows up, the hogs run right over and strike a pose." It soon became obvious that, despite the hogs, Willkie's main crop in Rushville was politics.

During their stay in Rushville, the Willkies lived in a three-story red brick house surrounded by a lawn, shaded by maple trees and within easy walking distance of the home of his wife's mother, Mrs. Cora Wilk. With his shirtsleeves rolled up, Willkie often sat out on the grass to hold informal press conferences. His campaign office on Main Street, between a drugstore and a grocery, on the second floor of a frame building owned by Mrs. Wilk, swarmed with secretaries, publicity men, writers, staff assistants, and some fifty reporters and photographers. Eight volunteers were needed to sort and handle three thousand letters a day; incoming messages made it necessary to put in seventeen additional telegraph lines; and phones rang with long distance calls from all over the country. For Willkie, it was like Colorado Springs all over again and at times even more hectic. There was a stream of visitors, both important and unimportant, and the inevitable interview and picture sessions.

By the summer of 1940, German U-boat attacks and other war actions had reduced Britain's fleet of destroyers to only sixty ships, and President Roosevelt began working out an agreement to trade Britain fifty old American destroyers that were in storage for the right to set up American military and naval bases in six of Britain's possessions in the Western Hemisphere. The President, through mutual friends, tried to persuade Willkie not to make a campaign issue of the plan. Willkie knew many Republicans would turn against him fiercely if he came to any secret agreement with the President on an action that was closer than anything before to active intervention in the war. Yet he firmly believed all possible aid should be given to Britain. He went as far as he could and privately agreed that he would not be against the idea of transferring destroyers but made it clear that he couldn't be expected to give advance approval to any specific plan that was worked out.

When President Roosevelt announced the destroyer deal to Congress as an accomplished fact, Willkie declared: "The country will undoubtedly approve the program to add to our naval and air bases and the assistance given Great Britain." But he added that "it is regrettable that the President did not deem it necessary to secure the approval of Congress or permit public discussion." As political pressure mounted, Willkie felt forced to charge that the agreement was "the most arbitrary and dictatorial action ever taken by a president." The result, as had happened so often throughout the campaign, was a blurring of Willkie's stand and confusion in the minds of voters. He was for trading destroyers to the British, but against doing it without public debate and congressional approval, just as he had been for many of the accomplishments of the New Deal but against what he felt were the "undemocratic methods" of achieving those goals. Many Americans failed to understand a philosophy that could approve the ends but not the means.

On September 12, he left Rushville for the start of an active campaign that was to make him the most widely traveled presidential candidate in American history. Within seven weeks, his campaign train would cover almost nineteen thousand miles in thirty-one states where he would deliver nearly five hundred brief talks and longer speeches, and would shake hands with tens of thousands of Americans. The first leg of the trip was to take him seven thousand miles in two weeks, through eighteen states to the Pacific and back. Coffeyville, Kansas, where he had been a high school teacher of history, was chosen as the place for the first major speech, but Willkie decided to talk his way to Coffeyville with a barnstorming tour through Illinois and Missouri.

While radio could carry his voice, there was no other way in those days before television to let the country see him, and his managers were counting heavily on his personal appeal to win votes. There were some gloomy predictions that the election was already lost before the real campaign began, but Willkie was convinced everything would swing his way once he had a chance to talk to the people directly, face to face.

Chapter Fourteen

THE *Willkie Special* started out from Rushville as a train of twelve cars, and grew to sixteen as it became not only a rolling hotel and office building but also a mobile chain of "smoke-filled rooms" into which politicians crowded by the carload between station stops.

Everybody wanted to talk to Willkie and almost all at once. Tickets to board the train had to be sent out in advance to party chairmen in each state it passed through, to be distributed to important guests, governors, senators, publishers, financial backers, and party candidates. Some who failed to exchange a few words with Willkie in person went away with their feelings hurt, but he managed to see an amazing number of his migratory visitors.

The Willkie family lived in a private car, called the *Pioneer*, at the rear of the train, where he spent forty-two nights during the campaign. Mrs. Willkie was with him through the entire ordeal, always at his side in public, gracious and cheerful, silent while she let him do the talking. Willkie's son Philip also shared his father's trials and triumphs during much of the trip, and his brother Ed was his right-hand man and buffer against unwanted intrusions. His other brothers, Bob and Fred, joined the family group at various times.

Closest to Willkie, aside from the family, was Russell Davenport, with whom he discussed all matters of policy and who took charge of the speech writing. Oren Root was another close adviser, and aboard the train as representatives of the party organization were Senator Taft's law partner, former Congressman John B. Hollister, and Indiana Congressman Charles Halleck. Handling the tough task of managing the entire train, its accommodations, visitor space, routes, and time schedules was New York lawyer Harold Gallagher, a trusted personal friend of Willkie's and later his law partner. Reporters described Gallagher as "the only man aboard who knew how to say no."

Willkie's press-secretary, Lem Jones, had held the same job with Dewey until two months before. He dealt with the seventy-five reporters who lived aboard the train and who had a special lounge car fitted out as a rolling newspaper office, as well as with the dozens of additional reporters who boarded the train at various stops along the way. Willkie's press relations were as informal as always. He relaxed with the reporters, sat around sharing jokes, snacks, and drinks with them, and asked them as many questions about the campaign as he answered. He spoke to them so freely, he sometimes revealed in advance things he planned to say in his next major speech so that it was old news by the time he delivered it. But there were always surprises that kept them on their toes, since in public he might say anything appropriate that happened to come to his mind at the moment, and they never could be sure how far he would depart from any prepared text.

His speech writing staff included, along with other specialists called upon from time to time, former *New York Times* financial writer Elliot Bell, Pierce Butler, Jr., who was head of the Democrats for Willkie and was the son of a Supreme Court justice, and Bartley Crum, a young liberal West Coast lawyer. Willkie would first talk over the idea for a speech with Russell Davenport, who would take notes. Then one or more speech writers would go to work, and Davenport would pull a rough draft together and submit it to Willkie for approval. Willkie would suggest changes and finally would edit the speech into his own style of words and phrases. But before the campaign was over, speeches had to be produced at such a rapid rate Willkie sometimes had no chance to read them before he stood up to deliver them.

The speech writers kept a twenty-man research staff working overtime aboard the train, one car of which was devoted entirely to the research department, with rows of filing cabinets so filled with material that the cabinets finally overflowed, and papers had to be stacked on the platform between cars. They were backed by an additional research and writing staff in New York, but even then, they frequently ran out of material. The writers were especially hard-pressed in their search for local color, historic facts, and humorous remarks that would fit each locality in which Willkie spoke.

Other cars housed a reference library, a communications and mailing center, secretaries, people to produce press releases, a darkroom for photographers, and a maze of typewriters, desks, cabinets, duplicating machines, and other equipment. Service people were required for cleaning, housekeeping, laundry, and meals. The hectic conditions under which the whole complex operated led reporters to affectionately dub the train the "Squirrel Cage." Certainly no other campaign train had ever been like the *Willkie Special*. Soon to become a thing of the past, as quickened air travel and television gave candidates easier ways to reach the people, it was the greatest of its kind. Stories about it have become political legend, such as the one of the girl reporter planted aboard as a spy for the Democrats, and of the Republican committeewoman who fell off the back platform when the train suddenly started to move on, just as she was about to make a speech.

But, for Willkie, the odyssey was serious and it hardly began before he nearly lost his voice. On his way to Coffeyville, the train's first stops were in the Chicago area. Four speeches were planned, but he raced around to deliver at least half a dozen talks during the day in addition to the planned ones. At breakfast time, hundreds of people crowded Chicago's Union Station to greet him. He was wildly cheered by thousands who jammed the streets and skyscraper windows of the financial and shopping districts, but workers at the Chicago stockyards received him less warmly, and his reception was mixed as he toured various big industrial plants, visited the suburbs, and addressed a rally of fifteen thousand Negroes gathered at the American Giants Baseball Park. During the day, an estimated one million people had seen and heard him but when the day was over, his voice was so hoarse he could hardly speak. Two Chicago specialists were hurried aboard the train to treat him.

At Rock Island, after only two days of the campaign trip, his throat was so bad he was able only to whisper to the crowd, "The spirit is willing but the voice is weak." Two scheduled talks were cancelled and under doctors' orders he was kept from trying to speak. A Hollywood throat specialist, Dr. Harold Barnard, was flown East to board the train. Over Sunday, with the doctor's help and enforced rest, Willkie got his voice back and agreed to depend more on microphones after that. Dr. Barnard stayed aboard the train and kept Willkie's voice more or less in working condition, and theatrical star Walter O'Keefe, who was in charge of

141

campaign entertainment, worked to improve his microphone technique.

Coffeyville, where he delivered his first major speech, welcomed him as an old friend. With many of his former high school students in the audience, Willkie spoke on "the preservation of democracy," and charged that President Roosevelt was trying to sell the American people "the gold brick of safety without sacrifice." The train rolled on to Tulsa, Oklahoma, to Amarillo, Texas, and then to Albuquerque, New Mexico. There he told an audience of fifteen thousand that while he wanted victory, his real campaign was for unity among all Americans. "I hope I win," he said, "but if I lose you will find me upholding the hands of the government at this critical time."

He had left the Midwest on Saturday, and by Wednesday night he was in California with his energy undiminished and his spirits high. When some heckler in a huge San Diego audience shouted, "Vote for Roosevelt!", Willkie grinned and shot back, "There you are, one man in a hundred thousand." In Los Angeles, he toured the great airplane factories, rode through streets so jammed with cheering people that he was unable to get to the steps of City Hall to speak, and that night, seventy-five thousand turned out to hear him at a rally staged as a colossal Hollywood spectacle.

The train moved up through the cities of California, with seven formal speeches and three times as many informal ones along the way. Willkie spoke about New Deal economics and taxation, recalled the 1932 Democratic campaign promise to reduce the cost of government by twenty-five per cent, and said that he hoped that the Democrats would remember their current pledges better than that. He jibed at President Roosevelt's "non-political" speeches and his refusal to debate the issues of the campaign directly. When a man in Tulare shouted, "I want a job!", Willkie answered, "You're just like 9,600,000 others in the United States who are crying for jobs. There's no reason we can't stimulate the economy to provide jobs for all."

In San Francisco, he again urged "aid to Britain, our first line of defense and our only remaining friend," called for economic help to China, the "asquisition and development of Pacific air bases," and American leadership in planning (while the war was on) the world that would be left after the war. "We must work for a higher standard of living, not only here in America," he said, "but in other countries as well."

After speeches in Portland and Seattle, and whistle-stopping through the states of Oregon and Washington, he began his long swing back toward the East. His voice, although sometimes hoarse, held out. In Missoula, Montana, a ten-year-old boy threw a tomato at him, one of a number of such incidents that later included the hurling of eggs, apples, cantaloupes, potatoes, burned out light bulbs, rocks, phone books, and even an office wastebasket and chair that were dumped from a skyscraper window. Fortunately, nobody was seriously hurt by any of the hoodlum barrages, and Willkie shrugged off most of them as part of the lunatic fringe that surrounds political campaigns.

In Madison, Wisconsin, where he spoke after talking his way through the Dakotas and Nebraska, he good-humoredly faced down a group of university students who tried to heckle him off the stage, appealed to their sense of fair play, and not only won a hearing but an ovation from the audience when he finished his speech. *Time* magazine reported that he "rose to an oratorical form that astounded the correspondents who were only now discovering that Willkie doesn't talk, he likes to argue." From Wisconsin, he went on to Iowa and completed the first two weeks by returning to Chicago. He had left many Democrats angry and many

143

Republicans disgruntled, but he and his campaign managers were generally pleased by the response. The most strenuous part of the campaign still lay ahead, but correspondents already were writing that no previous candidate in history, including William Jennings Bryan, had ever spoken in person to so many Americans.

Without pause, the campaign train took him to the Empire Race Track in Yonkers, New York, where 45,000 at the state Republican convention hailed his declaration that: "The time has come when the government must cease giving to the people. The time has come for the people to give to the government." Two days later he was back in the Midwest to start a swing through Michigan, Illinois, Ohio, and Pennsylvania. Deliberately he chose to enter some of the most thoroughly entrenched Democratic areas in the country where he knew feeling against him and the Republican party would run high. He was greeted with boos as often as cheers and with furious demonstrations, bombardments of fruits, vegetables, and eggs.

"Please, please, listen to what I have to say," he pleaded with angry crowds. "You must not close your minds. Listen to me on the radio, listen to the arguments on the other side, *then* decide how you want to vote."

He had tried to keep the campaign on a relatively high level, but others in both parties had made it what some newspapers were calling "the dirtiest political mud-throwing exhibition since the Civil War." Galling to him as he returned to the New York metropolitan area, to New Jersey, and the cities of New England were the continuing attempts to link him with extremist groups. Time after time he declared himself against "race hatred, bigotry and Hitlerism." He said he considered every anti-Semite "a possible traitor to America" and made the flat statement: "I repudiate any committee or individual who is supporting me on the basis of racial or religious prejudice." He angrily rejected the praise of one rabble-rouser by saying, "I don't want it. I don't have to be President of the United States but I do have to live with myself."

Willkie was particularly enraged when the Colored Division of the Democratic National Committee in New York circulated a pamphlet stressing his German ancestry, quoting Hitler's remarks about Negroes, and declaring that Willkie had been nominated "by the Hitler formula." He began to strike back. Under emotional stress and the pressure of politicians to make the campaign more dramatic, he lashed out at nearly everything President Roosevelt did, voiced the theme of the Republican platform that tried to brand the Democratic party as the "war party," and made some statements he himself later regretted. In St. Louis in mid-October, he received the greatest ovation of his campaign when he shouted to an audience of thousands: "We do not want to send our boys over there again and we do not intend to. If you elect me President, we will not. . . . I believe if you elect the third-term candidate they will be sent."

His new campaign tactics began to show results that worried the Democrats. As he barnstormed from the East to the Midwest and back, public opinion polls showed a gradual swing in his favor, a considerable jump in the possible votes he might capture. Crowds jammed the halls where he spoke, sometimes filled the streets for blocks around, and roared approval. President Roosevelt had continued to ignore Willkie's repeated calls for direct debate while his lieutenants did the campaigning. But messages and telegrams from Democrats in all parts of the country began to pour into the White House, as presidential aide, Samuel

Rosenman, later said, "warning that Willkie was making headway and that the President had better do some campaigning." As Eleanor Roosevelt wrote afterwards, the election was the one her husband was the least certain of winning, and while "Franklin had intended to make no speeches in this campaign except over the radio, he finally was persuaded to make a few."

On October 15, accusing the Republicans of "systematic and deliberate falsifications of fact," President Roosevelt announced that he would openly reply in a series of speeches. Giving up his stand of being above the political battle, he entered the fight with zest and in his first speech in Philadelphia declared, "I am an old campaigner and I love a good fight."

Willkie continued to make gains for the next few weeks, but President Roosevelt's active campaigning gradually but surely made his reelection certain. His familiar voice brought reassurance to millions of voters, reminded them of the benefits the New Deal had brought, tore apart Republican claims and charges, ridiculed Willkie's pledges and promises. With his great skill as an orator, Roosevelt sometimes gleefully and sometimes dramatically pointed to the nation's obvious economic progress since the Depression years, to its growing strength in national defense, and to the obstructions Republican isolationists had tried to put in the path of preparedness and aid to the European democracies.

Afterwards, Willkie said, "When I heard the President hang the isolationist votes on me and get away with it, I knew I was licked." But it was the emotional issue of staying out of the war that the President stressed most during the short time left in the campaign, and if Willkie had been reckless in claiming he alone could keep American boys from being sent to war, the President's answer also went farther than either of them honestly could foresee. "I have said this

146

before, but I shall say it again and again," the President declared. "Your boys are not going to be sent into any foreign wars."

During the last week of the campaign, Willkie made three or four speeches a day in New York and the Eastern states, and ended with a rally which drew twenty-three thousand roaring enthusiasts to New York's Madison Square Garden to hear his plea for the "preservation of democracy" that he called the "Battle of America." He pledged, if elected, a new national unity of all economic classes, races, creeds, and colors, "a unity that you have not had in the last eight years." Meanwhile, in Cleveland, President Roosevelt asked for a vote of confidence.

Both sides, as usual, claimed victory. Public opinion polls were divided, generally favoring Roosevelt but predicting a much closer contest than it turned out to be. On the morning of Election Day, Willkie privately told his press secretary, Lem Jones, that only a miracle could put him in the White House, but he went on believing in that miracle until the very end.

Willkie voted in a New York public school polling place and returned to his headquarters at the Commodore Hotel where he, his wife, and Philip had taken a private suite on the fourteenth floor. Early returns that evening were in his favor, but the trend was soon reversed, and the night became a long and dismal one as Willkie sat listening to the results in his room. Shortly after midnight he went down to the ballroom, where hundreds of admirers had gathered for what they hoped would be a victory celebration. Some were crying, all were dejected, and he tried to cheer them up. He told them: "Don't be afraid and never quit." Party leaders were admitting defeat, but Willkie went to bed shortly before two in the morning, still refusing to concede the election.

He won more votes than any Republican candidate in history and cut President Roosevelt's 1936 margin of victory almost in half, but carried only ten states while Roosevelt took the other thirty-eight. Willkie polled more than twenty-two million popular votes against more than twenty-seven million for Roosevelt, but in electoral votes Roosevelt's victory was even more overwhelming. The President swept almost every big city in the country with pluralities great enough to carry the important states, for a total of 449 electoral votes to only 82 for Willkie. Many top Democrats, as well as Republicans, later said that Willkie would have defeated any candidate except Roosevelt. The analyists went to work studying the returns, to play the traditional game of trying to guess why Americans voted as they did, but the best answer seemed to be that most people didn't want to trade a known Roosevelt for an unknown Willkie at a time when the nation faced critical years.

Willkie finally accepted the defeat with good grace, and in his telegram of congratulations to President Roosevelt the next morning he said: "I know that we are both gratified that so many Americans participated in the election. I wish you all personal health and happiness." Later in the morning, he made a short radio broadcast, thanking the millions who had voted for him and saying: "I accept the results of the election with complete good will. The popular vote shows the vitality of our democratic principles."

He and his family lunched at the Yale Club with friends who reported that he was "frank, cheerful, ready to admit his own political mistakes" and "showed no bitterness against F.D.R." After lunch the Willkies returned to the hotel to pick up some personal belongings and then took a taxi home to their Fifth Avenue apartment. "I'm not weeping," Mrs. Willkie told reporters. "We Willkies have a lot of buoyancy. You can't down us." She spoke of a vacation and a welcome return to private life. But Wendell Willkie's life was not about to become private. With the election behind him, he was about to begin his most important years in helping to shape America's policies and decisions regarding world problems.

Chapter Fifteen

Although he had lost the election, Wendell Willkie had gained an enormous popular following, and thousands of the Americans who had voted for him now sent telegrams and letters, urging him to continue in public life. He knew he still had great influence with the people, and he meant to use it.

Six days after the election, on Armistice Day, 1940, he made a nationwide radio address to urge his followers to form a "loyal opposition" to the Roosevelt administration. He called upon them for "vigorous, loyal and public-spirited" criticism of the administration when it seemed warranted, but warned them not to "fall into the partisan error of opposing things just for the sake of opposition." Theirs must not be merely an opposition against, he said, but "an opposition for—for a strong America."

He then took off with his wife for a six-weeks' vacation at Hobe Sound, Florida, where he said he was just going to "read, fish and rest." But while he was relaxing in the sun and turning down opportunities to become a university president, write a newspaper column or edit a national magazine, he reached a decision to try what hardheaded politicians said was impossible. He had come to the firm conclusion that the survival of democracy and freedom in the world hinged upon victory in Britain. He hoped to keep his leadership of the Republican party while he tried to put its strength behind a Democratic president in behalf of that belief.

Interrupting his vacation for a flying visit to New York to address the National Interfraternity Conference, Willkie made an urgent plea for America "to help the fighting men of Britain to preserve the rim of freedom which is constantly shrinking." At the same time, he pointed out that Americans had deep and honest differences of opinion on the question, and he urged free and full discussion and an end to name-calling. "It does no good to say of the man who believes that we must send help to that rim of freedom that he is a warmonger," he declared, "or of the man who believes that America should protect herself wholly within these shores that he's a Fifth Columnist or a Nazi or something else."

America's feelings against the Nazis hardened, and the swell of sympathy rose with each report of the horror of night bombing attacks. On December 29, in a radio address to the nation, President Roosevelt made his historic call for America to become "the great arsenal of democracy," declaring that "never since Jamestown and Plymouth Rock has our American civilization been in such danger as now." Alarmed by the speech, and by the message the President sent to Congress calling for America to supply the materials to defend democracy on a lend-lease basis to the Allies, isolationists were aroused to fury.

The Lend-Lease Bill, introduced into Congress on January 10, 1941, proposed to grant the President sweeping powers "notwithstanding the provisions of any other law" to authorize the "manufacture in arsenals, factories and shipyards

151

(of) any defense article for the government of any country whose defense the President deems vital to the defense of the United States," to repair, outfit and recondition such war supplies, to supply other governments with full information about them, and to "release for export any defense article to any such government." Such American materials and aid could be sold, transferred, exchanged, leased, loaned, or otherwise disposed of on any terms or conditions "which the President deems satisfactory."

Dewey, Taft, Vandenberg, former presidential candidate Landon, and former President Hoover immediately took a strong stand against the Lend-Lease Bill, along with many other Republicans and other Americans who attacked it as undemocratic and unconstitutional. Dewey charged it "would bring an end to free government in the United States." Taft declared that "it authorizes the President to make war on any nation in the world and to enter the present war if he wishes to do so, as he apparently does." Hoover warned Congress against what he called "the enormous surrender of its responsibilities." Landon assailed it as a step towards war and "a slick scheme to fool the taxpayers." Some were against it even though they favored restricted aid to the Allies, and others took a totally isolationist view. Congressman Hamilton Fish of New York predicted that Republicans in Congress would vote almost unanimously against the bill.

Willkie promptly endorsed lend-lease. His statement, although restrained, amounted to a rebuke of the top leaders of his own party who had attacked the proposal. "It is the history of democracy that under such dire circumstances extraordinary powers must be granted to the elected Executive," he said. "Democracy cannot hope to defend itself in any other way."

He expressed the hope that Republicans would not oppose granting such power to the Roosevelt administration "just because it is this administration" and reminded them that "the people chose this administration and we must abide by that choice." He also hoped that debate would "be confined to the merits of this bill" and that it would not become a quarrel between the two parties. Hitting directly at those who claimed they favored aid to Britain although they were against lend-lease, he warned that "lip-service friends of Britain will seek to sabotage the program of aid to Britain and her allies behind the screen of opposition to this bill."

Many Republicans, not only isolationists, were ready to call Willkie a traitor to the party. His answer was that he owed a duty to the nation that was greater than any obligation to the party alone, but that he also believed he was doing what was best for the party. "Let me say to you," he told a meeting of the Women's National Republican Club a few days later, "that if the Republican party in the year 1941 makes a blind opposition to this bill and allows itself to be presented to the American people as the isolationist party, it will never again gain control of the American government."

He put aside the written notes for his speech, and extemporaneously went on to voice one of the central beliefs of his life:

Whether we like it or not, America cannot remove itself from the world. Every development in the art of transportation, every development in the art of communication, has reduced the size of the world so that the world today actually is no larger than the thirteen original colonies were when we established our system of liberty in the United States.

And as much as we would like to withdraw within ourselves and as much as we would like to disregard the rest of the world—we cannot. We cannot forget the fighting men of Europe. They are defending our liberty as well as theirs. If they are permitted to fall, I say to you quite deliberately that I do not believe liberty can survive here. I take issue with all

153

who say that we can survive with freedom in a totalitarian world.

Alf Landon took the lead in a fresh round of Republican attacks against Willkie. "There is no essential difference between Mr. Willkie's position and Mr. Roosevelt's position, which is to go to war if necessary to help England win," Landon said. "If Mr. Willkie had revealed it before the Republican National Convention he would not have been nominated, and if Mr. Roosevelt had revealed it before the election, he would not have been reelected."

But outside the conservative Republican leadership, Willkie had many supporters. He went on making speeches and statements on behalf of lend-lease and aid to Britain, and on January 12 called reporters to his office for a dramatic announcement that captured headlines and took everybody by surprise. After joking a bit about the election while he munched a ham sandwich, he casually told the reporters he was going to fly to wartime England in person to find out about conditions there, firsthand.

The inspiration had come to him while he was writing a magazine article, he said, and he had picked up the phone to call the State Department and find out whether he could get a passport. Secretary of State Hull had invited him to come down to Washington for a full briefing, and President Roosevelt had welcomed the idea, inviting him to come to the White House to talk it over if he wished. "I'm deeply appreciative," Willkie said. "I'll be glad to talk to the President."

Willkie's conferences in Washington were scheduled for the day before President Roosevelt's inauguration as the first third-term president in history and many visitors who had crowded into the city for the Inaugural also flocked to see Willkie. Hundreds jammed the entrance to the building where he and Secretary Hull talked for nearly two hours,

154

and when Hull accompanied him to the White House there was another waiting crowd. Willkie's arrival also caused a flurry among the White House staff, according to Mrs. Roosevelt, who wrote that "the household was so anxious to get a glimpse of him while he sat waiting in Franklin's study on the second floor that suddenly many people had errands that took them down the hall."

It had been three years since Willkie's last meeting with the President, when neither of them had known they would fight a political battle for the right to occupy the Executive Mansion. They greeted each other cordially, and President Roosevelt laughingly told the group he wished "Wendell" were going to be out on that cold inaugural stand the next day taking the oath of office instead of himself. Willkie jokingly answered that the President might want to trade places and go over to England.

They then retired for a private talk that, according to the later memoirs of various presidential aides, was relaxed, friendly, and unusually frank. What they said was not revealed except for Willkie's comment that they "talked of many things involved in the growing crisis and particularly of American production schedules," but their conversation apparently also reached the personal level of freely discussing some of the burdens of any man who must occupy the White House. Afterwards, Willkie described the meeting as "delightful," and the President remarked to a close associate that he had found himself liking Willkie more than he had expected to and that he was a "very good fellow."

President Roosevelt asked him to deliver a brief handwritten note to Prime Minister Churchill and in it he wrote: "Wendell Willkie will give you this. He is truly helping to keep politics out over here." The President's note included a verse by Henry Wadsworth Longfellow, which he told Churchill "applies to you as it does to us":

155

Sail on, O Ship of State!
Sail on, O Union strong and great!
Humanity with all its fears,
With all the hopes of future years,
Is hanging breathless on thy fate!

Willkie flew out of New York the morning of January 22 as a private citizen, paying his own way, and making it clear that he had no official status. He was going as an individual named Wendell Willkie, he said, to "see, hear and learn" all he could about Britain at war, and "I am representing no one." He intended to gather the facts about what Britain had and what it needed in war materials, how fast they were being produced and how much the bombings had hurt, and also to learn what thoughts and plans leaders might have about shaping the world after victory had been won. When reporters asked what practical use he would make of his information, he smiled and said, "I do make speeches and write sometimes."

The real purpose of the trip was to influence public opinion by personally dramatizing the link between the two great nations in democracy's struggle to survive, and by telling Britain's story to the people of the United States in a way that would stir the imagination of the average citizen as no amount of wordy debate ever would. In his flight to England there was the implied pledge that America truly would become the "arsenal of democracy" if other Americans would join him in backing lend-lease, and in understanding that "the fighting men of Europe are defending our liberty as well as theirs."

He flew by way of the Azores and Portugal, where he stopped to talk to Prime Minister Salazar, and reached England late on Sunday, January 26. His first London press conference the next morning attracted two hundred reporters, and although he protested that he had come "to listen and not to make speeches," almost everything he did in England from that moment on was reported in the world's newspapers. But throughout his visit he did stick to a polite refusal to discuss any official relationships, policies or politics, reminding newsmen that he was in no position to speak for the American government or for the man who had been elected president instead of himself.

After a conference with Foreign Minister Anthony Eden, he had his first talk with Churchill during a Monday luncheon at Chequers, the Prime Minister's official country residence, where he also met Mrs. Churchill and "was too interested in talking to notice what we ate." Churchill later commented that "every arrangement was made by us, with the assistance of the enemy, to let him see all he desired of London at bay." Their conversation lasted nearly two hours, and Churchill described Willkie as a "most able and forceful man" and one whose faith in Britain's ability to survive its ordeal of fire was "immensely heartening." Willkie found Churchill's courage and "large comprehension" inspiring, and thought that never in history was any man "more ideally suited to the particular task he was called on to perform."

Back at his hotel that afternoon, Willkie held two more press conferences, talked to presidential assistant Harry Hopkins whom the President had asked him to see while he was in England, met with British railroad and labor officials, and finished his first day by touring the bombed-out center of London. During the rest of his stay, arrangements were made for him to meet with almost everybody of importance he wished to see. He talked to nearly all the members of the British cabinet, leaders of the opposition parties, church dignitaries, bank governors, financiers, production, information and security chiefs, admirals, writers, philosophers, business executives, and heads of various governments in exile.

157

He visited air-raid shelters, cathedrals, and inspected invasion defenses, sat in on a stormy session of the House of Commons during a heated debate over wartime press censorship, and called the proceedings "the most dramatic example of democracy at work anybody could wish to see." Shocked by the sight of a street of bombed-out bookstores where three million volumes had been burned, he said, "They have destroyed the place where truth was told."

Forced into one shelter during an air raid, he was "very deeply moved" by the quiet human courage he saw all around him. "I'm a tough old egg, I think," he said, "but I am almost spilling over." He was as much impressed by the "calm, precise, magnificently efficient turning of your wheels of industry." Everywhere he went he had praise for "the spirit of the British people" and repeatedly told them and the world that "no nation was ever more united in a cause than England is united now." He said: "I like your nerve."

If his visit became "a love affair with England," as one commentator put it, the genuine affection was fully returned by the British people. They loved his naturalness, bluff cheerfulness, and lack of pretension. As the *London Times* said, Willkie's "sincerity, friendship, boundless energy and radiant high spirits" were a "tonic" wartime Britain needed. People gathered around him on the streets, massed in crowds to cheer him, shouted his name, sometimes burst into the singing of patriotic songs, sought his autograph on everything from a ukulele to a package of tea. He talked to policemen, soldiers, cab drivers, porters, air raid wardens, accepted spur-of-the-moment invitations to step into homes, shops and offices to say hello, met average families and shared cigarettes or coffee with them.

He appeared unexpectedly in a neighborhood tavern, played a game of darts, bought a round of drinks for the soldiers who were there, and exchanged banter with a pretty

158

barmaid. Walking past another place where a workman was repairing a bomb-damaged roof, Willkie shouted up, "Hey! What do *you* think of the war? Do you want to keep on fighting?" The roofer called back, "Well, Hitler isn't dead yet, is he?" When one elderly woman caught his arm to stop him on the street and cried, "We can take it! You go home and tell them that," Willkie answered, "I certainly will."

From London he went on to Dover, Birmingham, Coventry —where the Germans had made their first attempt to destroy an entire city by indiscriminate night bombing—and then to Liverpool and Manchester, and everywhere was feted, mobbed, all but swept off his feet. Men broke police lines to grip his hand, and women burst forward impulsively to hug or kiss him.

Meanwhile, Nazi broadcasts aimed at Britain pumped out a chorus of propaganda attacks against him, questioning his German ancestry. Willkie replied by recording messages to be broadcast to Germany by the British, stressing the fact that his grandfather had left Germany in 1848 to protest against a military autocracy similar to that of Hitler's, and declaring that "the great majority of my fellow countrymen of German descent reject and hate the aggression and lust for power of the present German government." His statements were later printed in leaflets dropped by British fliers over Germany.

Willkie interrupted his visit to England to fly to Dublin for a long talk with Prime Minister De Valera in a fruitless attempt to persuade the Irish leader to change his policy of strict neutrality, and then flew back to London the same afternoon for tea with England's king and queen. For a visit with royalty, it was an unusually informal one, during which they joked and talked freely, and Willkie was impressed by the queen's simple manner and keen sense of humor.

As he prepared to leave for the flight that would bring him

back to the United States after having been away eighteen days, he told reporters that "to say I am staggered" by the way the British people had received him "would be putting it mildly." It was, he said, "the experience, the thrill of a lifetime." In his final statement before leaving, he said: "Any thing I can do in America to help Britain in her fight for freedom, I certainly shall do." The *London Pictorial* commented that "Mr. Willkie's great fact-finding trip has earned more newspaper, radio and newsreel space than almost anything else in the war."

But at home, some Republicans were calling it a "one-man circus," and as the debate over lend-lease came to a boil so did the enmity of many of the conservative leaders of his party. They accused him of "unnecessary cooperation" with President Roosevelt. A group of Young Republicans tried to get a national meeting in Des Moines to adopt a resolution charging that the party was "deliberately sabotaged by a candidate of the Democratic faith." At another meeting in Omaha of party leaders from sixteen Midwestern states, a revolt against Willkie's leadership was barely held in check.

While he was on his way back, the House of Representatives passed the Lend-Lease Bill, but with 135 Republicans voting against it and with the real showdown still to come in the Senate. When his plane touched down for a stop at Trinidad, there was a cable awaiting him from a man Willkie never identified except as "one of the leaders of the American isolationist movement," warning that "my reputation would be the subject of debasement in every town in America if I carried out my intention of testifying."

The day Willkie reached New York, February 9, Winston Churchill delivered one of his great speeches in a dramatic plea for aid, in which he referred to Willkie as "a great champion" and asked America to "give us the tools and we will finish the job." Two days later, Willkie went to Washing-

ton to testify in favor of lend-lease before the Senate Foreign
Relations Committee, and to try to make a reality of the national unity on foreign policy that his speeches and his trip
to England had pledged.

A long line began to form at the door of the Senate caucus
room before seven in the morning although the hearings
weren't due to start for another three hours, and Willkie
wouldn't appear until mid-afternoon. Some eighteen hundred people finally jammed into the room that had seats for
less than a third that many while hundreds more remained
standing outside. In the seats were nearly all the members of
the Senate, nearly half the members of the House, many
Cabinet members and top agency officials. Others were
forced to kneel or sit on the floor, and newspapers reported
that nothing like such a crowd had ever been seen before at
any Senate hearing. Over at the White House, when reporters turned up for their regular news conference with
President Roosevelt, he told them, "You're at the wrong end
of Pennsylvania Avenue today."

Willkie's testimony dramatically was kept until last, after
a lengthy parade of witnesses for and against the measure.
He read his statement calmly, in a quiet voice, arguing again
for a reasonable approach to the issue. In temperate language, he explained his reasons for rejecting the isolationist
point of view and noted that some who were against the bill
said they were for restricted aid to Britain, but he argued,
"If we are going to adopt a policy of aid to Britain, it is
necessary above all to make that aid effective."

He then urged the adoption of lend-lease, the release to
Britain of all American bombers not needed for training
purposes, and the sending to Britain of from five to ten
American destroyers a month. Warning that no man could
guarantee that aid to Britain would not involve the nation in
war, he said that the alternative of being surrounded by

161

totalitarian powers and threatened by dictators whose desire was for conquest was too great to risk. "If we are to avoid such a calamity, we must now have courage," he said. "We must bravely do the things which we know ought to be done. And we must lay the moral, intellectual and spiritual foundations for the kind of a world we want our children to inherit, a world in which America will share with other nations the responsibilities of peace."

Under the hammering cross-examination of opponents of lend-lease, Willkie adroitly handled most of the loaded questions fired at him. One after another, his questioners brought up statements he had made during the election campaign, trying to embarrass him and prove he had been insincere. Senator Bennett Clark of Missouri quoted things Willkie had said about President Roosevelt's leading the nation toward war, and Willkie answered, "I made a great many statements about him. He was my opponent, you know. In campaigns, we all expand a bit. I don't see any reason for raking up these old acrimonies."

Senator Clark persisted, and Willkie protested again against raking over old campaign statements. "I struggled as hard as I could to beat Franklin Roosevelt and I tried to keep from pulling my punches," he said. "He was elected President. He is my President now. I expect to disagree with him whenever I please." His answer brought such prolonged applause from the spectators that the chairman threatened to clear the room. North Dakota's Senator Nye then tried to pin Willkie down to one specific quotation against the President from one of his campaign speeches, and Willkie finally grinned and honestly admitted, "It was a bit of campaign oratory."

There was delighted laughter, soon echoed across the country by newspaper editorials that praised his honesty in sweeping aside the pretension that everything said in political campaigns must be accepted as enduring truth. "I think it was one of the most courageous things any man has ever said in public life," editor William Allen White wrote. "It was not discreet, but it was deeply honest." But although Willkie meant the remark to apply to the one particular campaign quotation he had been asked about, his political enemies turned it to everything he said. It plagued Willkie from then on. No matter how sincere he was, opponents charged that he was indulging again in "campaign oratory."

The Senate hearing ended with news commentators predicting that after Willkie's appearance there was no longer any serious doubt about the passage of lend-lease. He went from the caucus room to the White House to talk for an hour and a half with President Roosevelt. The next day was Lincoln's Birthday, a traditional day for Republican gatherings, and Willkie spoke to the National Republican Club in New York. After once more urging speedy and adequate aid to Britain, he talked of "the real faith that the American people worship most, not partisanship, nor bitterness, nor vindictiveness in their party leaders, but love of mankind and tolerance and understanding," and warned that Republicans must not be "merely those who find fault and who in one of the great critical moments of history find nothing nobler than compromise."

But at Republican gatherings in other cities, many Republican conservatives used the occasion to attack Willkie. Senator Taft declared that "Mr. Willkie does not and cannot speak for the Republican party." Senator Nye called his endorsement of lend-lease "a betrayal." While public opinion polls showed that Willkie's popularity with the general public was near an all-time peak, it was near an all-time low among party bosses. Columnist Raymond Clapper wrote: "Wendell Willkie is the hated target of most of the influential politicians in the Republican party today. They are

163

conspiring to get rid of him. They hate him more than they hate Mr. Roosevelt."

Senate debate on lend-lease was long, and the Republican attacks from the floor against Willkie were so bitter that a Democrat, Senator Prentiss Brown of Michigan, finally rose to his defense. "I wish to say that evidently the gentleman from Indiana who ran on the Republican ticket is the most unpopular Republican in the country in the United States Senate," Brown said, "and probably the most popular Republican in the country outside the United States Senate."

Finally, on March 8, the Senate passed the bill, by sixty votes to thirty-one, and included in it many of Willkie's recommendations. Three days later, when the final vote on the modified bill was taken in the House, nearly two-thirds of the Republicans voted in favor of lend-lease.

President Roosevelt signed it immediately, and five minutes later approved the first transfers of war material to Britain. The President later was quoted by a close associate, playwright Robert Sherwood, as saying that "we might not have had lend-lease or selective service or a lot of other things if it hadn't been for Wendell Willkie. He was a godsend to the country when we needed him most."

Columnist Walter Lippmann was to write: "Historians will say, I believe, that second only to the Battle of Britain, the sudden rise and nomination of Willkie was the decisive event, perhaps providential, which made it possible to rally the free world when it was almost conquered. Under any other leadership but his, the Republican party would have turned its back upon Great Britain, causing all who still resisted Hitler to feel that they were abandoned."

Chapter Sixteen

Pᴿɪᴠᴀᴛᴇ citizen Wendell Willkie, the holder of no public office, probably influenced the policies and decisions of the United States as much as any one man except President Roosevelt himself during the crucial nine months from the passage of lend-lease to the Japanese attack on Pearl Harbor. He not only backed the President step by step in each major move toward preparedness but on some measures took a stand ahead of the President to pave the way.

As much as any former candidate for the presidency could, he tried to put aside all personal politics and urged other leaders of both parties to do the same. With civilization facing the crisis of totalitarian conquest, he said, "talk of party politics is completely out of place in either party." He was a leading political figure, of course, and remained among likely future presidential candidates, but time after time he rejected what was politically expedient to stand instead for what he believed was right. He told an interviewer in the spring of 1941: "If I could write my own obituary and I had a choice between saying I had been an unimportant

President or a person who had contributed to saving democracy at a critical moment, I'd prefer the latter."

As a private citizen, he took up the practice of law again, as senior partner of a firm that became Willkie, Owen, Farr, Gallagher and Walton, and moved into offices on the twenty-seventh floor of a building in New York's downtown financial district with a view of the harbor and the Statue of Liberty. There he continued to receive several thousand letters a day, more invitations to speak than any man could accept, and requests to endorse movements and causes and to lend his name and influence to about everyone and everything. "I am but an individual," he wrote a friend. "I have only so much time. In addition, I have to earn a living. . . ."

Somehow, despite the pressure of national events, he did manage to do a considerable amount of legal work for his firm, take an active interest in New York civic groups, and attend literary functions, concerts, ball games, and prize fights. A leader in the drive for relief funds for the people of China, he also flew to Canada to advance Canadian-American unity in a series of speeches, and fought for civil liberties on a dozen homefronts. He was a working director of Freedom House, which he had helped establish with a group of other prominent Americans as an outgrowth of citizen organizations that rallied to "defend America by aiding the Allies."

While he had little time to spend in his Fifth Avenue apartment, he cherished the evenings he could be there with his family and close friends, and also the brief trips he was able to make to his Rushville farms. Like thousands of other American parents, he felt both concern and pride when his son Philip entered the Navy.

Willkie wasn't alone in battling the isolationists. Millions of Americans were on his side, and the cause had many other able spokesmen. His opponents in both political parties also were formidable. They included honest and dedicated men who believed that Willkie and others like him were unnecessarily leading the United States into war. But on both sides there were some extremists and rabble-rousers who turned increasingly to the weapons of hate and personal slander. If Willkie had become among the most admired men in America, he certainly also was among the most hated. Missouri's Senator Clark called him "the undisputed leader of the war party in the United States," while President Roosevelt praised him as a leader who was showing "in word and action what patriotic Americans mean by rising above partisanship and rallying to the common cause."

He wrote magazine articles, issued press statements, spoke on the radio, and all through the spring, summer, and fall of 1941 made as many as three major speeches a week, crusading for national unity against the world aggression of Germany and Japan. He spoke in Pittsburgh and in Nashville, addressed a great Freedom Rally in New York's Madison Square Garden, a parading crowd at Columbus Circle, flew to the Midwest to speak to thousands in the Chicago stadium, and on across the country to lead a rally at the Hollywood Bowl, and another in San Francisco. He was denounced, slandered, threatened, and picketed, but also was cheered by great crowds.

His crusade became more than merely a battle against the isolationists. As Hitler's forces invaded Yugoslavia, took control of the Balkans and dominated the seas with Nazi submarines, and as the British in North Africa were driven back to the Egyptian border with heavy losses, he tried to make the American people face what he considered the fact that the United States already was in a state of undeclared war and had to take risks for its common defense with the Allies. He helped push public opinion forward, sometimes more boldly than President Roosevelt, who was limited by

167

his official position; and working with the President, he helped prepare the ground for some of Roosevelt's decisive acts. "There is no compromise," Willkie said. "The world will be dominated by free men or it will be dominated by enslaved men. We cannot appease the forces of evil. We cannot make peace with those who seek to destroy our way of life."

In April 1941, in advance of any position President Roosevelt then felt ready to take, Willkie demanded that lend-lease supplies be convoyed across the Atlantic under the protection of American warships to keep materials sent to Britain from being sunk by Nazi submarines. He argued that it was no longer enough for America to produce the materials of war for Britain. "It is now not only our job to produce the goods necessary for her survival," he said, "but to deliver them by whatever means will be most efficient."

It was a month later that President Roosevelt declared America's determination to deliver the goods to Britain when he proclaimed a "national emergency" after the sinking of an American freighter by a German U-boat. Declaring the need to maintain "freedom of the seas," the President revealed that the Nazis were sinking merchant ships twice as fast as combined British and American shipyards could produce them, and said, "I believe the delivery of needed supplies to Britain to be imperative."

Willkie praised the President for his "great message that has stirred the whole world," but continued to insist that the steps taken were not enough and that full convoy protection was needed. On July 7, President Roosevelt took the first step toward putting convoys into operation over part of the supply route when American troops occupied Iceland at the invitation of that country. The Navy was given the duty of keeping open the freedom of the seas to that point more than halfway to Britain.

Invited to lunch with the President at the White House, Willkie announced his full support of the occupation of Iceland. He said, "It was the clear intention of the founders of this country that in emergencies the President should lead." And he personally assured the President that despite the outcry of some Republicans in Congress, the decision on Iceland had the overwhelming approval of most of the country's Republican voters.

However, fifteen elder Republican statesmen, including Landon and Hoover, issued a manifesto demanding that Congress put a stop to what was called "the step by step projection of the United States into an undeclared war." It was followed by a caucus of Republican members of Congress who condemned "all executive acts and proceedings which might lead to war without the authorization of the Congress."

Willkie ignored both statements, but, in a speech in Los Angeles, expressed his own belief that the real danger was not in the acts of the President, but in the failure of Congress to act for preparedness. "We may be in danger if senators, instead of debating the real issues of this time, turn to personal invective," he said. "We may be in danger if congressmen become politically timid."

When the production of planes and other war material lagged, and some business leaders protested against government requests to cut back the output of civilian goods because it would interfere with "business as usual," Willkie said the national emergency required "the organization of our whole country into one vast, closely coordinated machine, with every part adjusted to every other part and the whole thing ticking like a first-class watch. It can be done and it must be done." He called upon the Government for the immediate setting up of a master production plan "with our industrial capacity allocated among our military, our naval,

169

aeronautical, lend-lease and civilian needs through a centralized authority under one man responsible to the President."

He took on the defense of the motion picture industry against isolationist charges that by producing several anti-Fascist films it was "spreading war propaganda." Some isolationists had appealed to prejudice in making the charge by claiming that Hollywood was trying to lead America into war against Hitler because most of the movie industry's leaders were Jewish. Willkie denounced such statements as "the most un-American talk made in my time" and said that "if the American people permit race prejudice to arise at this crucial moment they little deserve to preserve democracy."

A senate investigation of the movie industry was launched by Chairman Burton K. Wheeler of the Senate Interstate Commerce Committee, a leader of the isolationist Democrats who had charged that Willkie "and his little claque of Wall Street bankers, together with the motion picture industry, are trying to stir up sentiment to take us into war." Wheeler claimed the movie companies had ordered employees to attend Willkie's Hollywood Bowl speech and said, "Democrats follow Wendell Willkie, whom they were denouncing a few months ago. He is making their policies. He is telling them what to do. He is pushing the President."

When the Montana senator named a subcommittee to investigate the movies, Willkie promptly announced that he would act as counsel for the Motion Picture Producers and Distributors of America. He immediately put the Senate investigators on the defensive by sending a public letter to the chairman, raising the issue of freedom of speech and warning that any attempt to limit the freedom of expression in the movies was just a small step away from limiting all freedom of the press, "and the freedom of the individual to say what he believes." Questioning the legal authority of the Senate group, he said that if its purpose was to learn whether the movie industry was against Hitler, "there need be no investigation" for "we abhor everything which Hitler represents."

He hurried to Hollywood for conferences with producers who were to testify. Some of them thought the industry should play down the whole controversy, but Willkie urged them not to be intimidated. When the Washington hearings finally got underway, they produced a lot of sensational publicity but no evidence of any "propaganda conspiracy." The senators tried to silence Willkie by denying him the right to cross-examine witnesses, but they couldn't stop him from talking to the newspapers.

Willkie protested that the hearings were a farce and a "foolish show" being staged by isolationists to divert attention "from the real object of the investigation—the sabotage of the country's foreign policy." The hearings gradually faded to a halt and the events of war produced far more serious issues for Americans to face, but Willkie's part in them won him the lasting friendship of some of Hollywood's executives and eventually led to his becoming chairman of the board of Twentieth Century-Fox Films and a power in the movie capital.

When the occupation of Iceland was followed by the Atlantic Charter and its call for "the final destruction of Nazi tyranny," after the dramatic mid-August meeting at sea between Roosevelt and Churchill, the American challenge to Hitler produced increased Nazi submarine activity. Early in September, the American destroyer *Greer* was attacked by a German submarine on its way to Iceland, and within the month two American freighters were sunk, along with two more American-owned ships flying the flag of Panama. President Roosevelt ordered the Navy to "shoot on sight" any

German submarine that was encountered and not to wait for them to "strike their deadly blow first." And Willkie said: "The President has spoken as he should have spoken. He could not yield on such a fundamental right. This is the time for all Americans to rally to his support."

Willkie again took a position beyond that which President Roosevelt was prepared to take on the repeal of the Neutrality Act that had been passed in 1939 to limit American actions that might involve the country in war. The President said he regretted ever having approved the Neutrality Act and he urged the Congress to repeal it. Told by congressional leaders that full repeal would be impossible, the President compromised in October and asked Congress for a piecemeal revision of the law to remove the ban against the arming of merchant ships. He also hoped there might be early consideration of another section of the law which kept American ships out of the ports of nations at war. That was as far as President Roosevelt felt he could go without risking the possibility of a Republican revolt in Congress similar to the one that had stopped President Wilson's program in 1918.

But Willkie demanded outright repeal of the whole Neutrality Act, not merely revision of parts of it. He called upon the Republican party, which included leading opponents of repeal, to take the leadership in fighting to repeal it. "This must be done. It must be done for the sake of freedom. It must be done for the sake of America," Willkie said, "and to put it on the narrowest grounds it must be done for the sake of the Republican party. There is no longer any possible excuse for the continuance of tactics which, however applicable in times of peace, are indulged in at the expense of the people's safety in times of emergency."

His action both helped and embarrassed the President. *New York Times* columnist Arthur Krock described Willkie as "the follower who got ahead of the leader." Many congressional Republicans were outraged, but Willkie took his opponents by surprise and persuaded three Republican senators to introduce an amendment to the President's compromise bill that called instead for outright Neutrality Act repeal. He then released a statement signed by 124 prominent Republicans, including six governors, ten former governors and twenty-six members of the party's national committee, in support of his move. It amounted to a minority report and Willkie's tactics had little effect upon his Republican opponents in Congress, but the moves did spur the Democrats into action. Instead of asking for the piecemeal revision, the Democrats immediately introduced a resolution to wipe out almost the entire Neutrality Act.

His enemies in Congress were furious in striking back at Willkie. They disavowed him as the party's leader, charged that he was "just a stooge for President Roosevelt" and that "the President is going too slow for him," called him "a Trojan Horse who is trying to split the Republican party wide open," and the "Dr. Jekyll and Mr. Hyde of American politics." Landon criticized him at the Senate hearings, Taft took to the Senate floor to denounce him for advocating a "war policy," and Senator Nye charged he was Roosevelt's "little Sir Echo."

A group of House Republicans organized an attempt to read him out of the party for "trying to tell lifelong Republicans what to do." Representative Dewey Short of Missouri, leader of the anti-Willkie move, delivered a violent twenty-minute attack against him in the House that was roundly applauded by fellow Republicans. Short assailed Willkie as "this imposter, this Fifth Columnist, this preposterous man" and called him a "belligerent, bombastic, bellicose, bombinating blow-hard who couldn't be elected dog-catcher" and who was "unfit to lead any party."

173

Newspaper columnists, many of whom had praised Willkie for his "bold and courageous stand," commented that never in history had there been such a furious display of hatred by a party's congressional leaders against the man who had been the party's nominee for President exactly one year before. Willkie took the attack calmly, said it sounded like the last gasp of the "dying cause" of isolationism, and as for Representative Short: "His personal references remind me of a bad boy who, when he runs out of arguments, begins to make faces."

Congress voted to repeal the Neutrality Act, but most Republicans in both the House and Senate opposed repeal to the end. It would have failed in the House if twenty-two Republicans had not joined Democrats in voting for it. Only days before America's entrance into the Second World War, less than twelve per cent of the Republicans in Congress had supported Willkie's aggressive policy toward Germany and Japan.

More than a month before, Willkie had warned in speaking of Asia, "Let us not delude ourselves. Berlin, Tokyo and Rome are linked by the dangerous dream of world conquest. We must abandon the hope of peace." For weeks, Willkie had been considering a trip to Australia and New Zealand to study Far Eastern conditions now menaced by Japan, and to publicize American relations with those countries, as he had with Britain. He and President Roosevelt had talked over the project, and the President dictated a letter to him on December 5, offering to make any official arrangements Willkie desired. The President wrote that the trip would be "of great value to cement our relations with New Zealand and Australia not only now but in the future." He then said, "There is always the Japanese matter to consider. The situation is definitely serious. Perhaps the next four or five days will decide . . ."

On December 7, the Japanese struck at Pearl Harbor.

When the President's letter to Willkie arrived, it had a post-script added in hurried longhand: "This was dictated Friday morning—long before this vile attack started."

Peace finally had ended, war was declared, and on December 10, Willkie answered the President's letter, saying that obviously any immediate plans for the trip would have to be reconsidered but that he would be in Washington within the next few days and would like to talk to the President about how he could best serve in the emergency. Friends of the President had been making suggestions that Willkie join the administration in some top level government job. Willkie hoped to explain that while he was ready to serve in any capacity the emergency demanded, he felt it would be better not to take a place in the government.

He and the President met for lunch at the White House on December 15 for a "completely frank talk," and when reporters asked Willkie afterwards about rumors that he might join the Roosevelt administration he said no government position was in prospect at the moment. Months before, the President had offered to make him chairman of the Defense Labor Board but Willkie had declined. Later the President had talked to aides about putting Willkie in charge of war production or in various other positions. But probably both men finally decided there was more to be lost than gained if Willkie held a government position. He would lose his influence in the Republican party, leave the party liberals without a leader, and would sacrifice the value of his independence of the Roosevelt administration.

Willkie was at the White House again on January 13, 1942, this time not only to talk to the President but to renew his acquaintance with another White House visitor, Prime Minister Churchill. He and the President continued to meet every month or so for talks about many things connected with the war effort, and they exchanged frequent notes.

With the coming of the war, Willkie at last saw his

formula for national unity materialize. Most isolationists joined with other Americans in the common effort to stand united behind the Government, whatever past differences over international policy had been. If isolationism wasn't dead, it was at least in recess until it became revived again after the war with the new name of *nationalism.* There was also a temporary truce in party politics. It didn't last long, but Willkie's "loyal opposition" did become a working method for political harmony in the immediate emergency after Pearl Harbor.

Chapter Seventeen

W^{ITH} the United States just entering the war, Wendell Willkie looked ahead to the end of the war, determined to do what he could to keep history from repeating itself. He had always felt that one of history's great tragedies was America's rejection of Woodrow Wilson's League of Nations. While the country was united in war, he meant to harden public opinion so firmly in favor of a world union of nations that nothing again could shake the determination of the United States to be part of it. He also meant to put the leadership of the Republican party so fully on record for international cooperation that it could never retreat. Driven by that purpose, he devoted his writing, his speeches, and himself to it, greatly at the cost of his own political future.

"We must never forget what we are fighting for," he said. "We are fighting for the elimination from this world of narrow nationalism and isolationism, which are the breeders of war and of economic degradation and of poverty." He argued that if America had chosen international cooperation after the First World War, "the world would have been very different today" and "the Second World War might have been forestalled," but that we were "paying the bitter price for our worship of expediency, our endless seeking of the easy way out." America must help create a world where "there shall be equality of opportunity for every race and every nation," he said. "The end is freedom and freedom is indivisible. We cannot keep freedom to ourselves. If we are to have freedom we must share freedom."

In April 1942, against the determined opposition of many of its members, Willkie convinced the National Committee of the Republican party to go on record favoring cooperation with other nations after the war. The resolution he fought through to adoption, at the cost of arousing his enemies within the party to even greater resentment, declared in the name of the National Committee that:

> We realize that after this war, the responsibility of the nation will not be circumscribed within the territorial limits of the United States; that our nation has an obligation to assist in bringing about understanding, comity, and cooperation among the nations of the world in order that our own liberty may be preserved and that the blighting and destructive processes of war may not again be forced upon us and upon the free and peace-loving peoples of the earth.

The New York Times called it "the strongest and boldest statement of Republican foreign policy made in all these barren years." Willkie himself hailed the declaration as an abandonment by the party of isolationism, and a recognition of the necessity for the United States to assume a positive position in world affairs.

In almost the same breath, Willkie said that "the next job for Republicans to do is to see to it that in the coming primaries candidates are nominated who have the courage to declare and who sincerely believe these principles." He turned his own attention to New York, where Thomas E. Dewey was almost assured the Republican nomination for the governorship, and let it be known that he personally had serious doubts as to whether Dewey was the man the party should choose. Publicly he denied that he was leading a "stop-Dewey" movement, but made it clear that he would prefer almost any other candidate. He tried to prod Dewey into making a definite and unqualified statement in support of postwar world cooperation, saying he was puzzled by what he considered Dewey's wavering views on the question.

Several "draft-Willkie" movements were started to get Willkie himself to oppose Dewey for the New York governorship. Some of his close friends urged the move upon him, and newspapers commented that "Willkie is wrestling with the toughest decision of his political life," and saw a behind-the-scenes battle for control of the party between the Old Guard and the followers of Willkie which would determine the Republican choice of a 1944 presidential candidate. But on July 2, Willkie firmly and finally put an end to the speculation, after having aroused the everlasting antagonism of Dewey's supporters, and of the man who was to become among the most powerful in the party.

"I have no intention of becoming a candidate," Willkie said. "I am attempting to bring about the adoption of certain principles by the Republican party and the development of a type of leadership that will win the confidence of the American people. If I can accomplish these suggestions, other people can have every office in the United States, as far as I am concerned."

He was about to begin the most dramatic journey of his life, a trip that in fifty days would take him to five continents and over 31,000 miles of the world at war. He meant to bring home to Americans, as an individual citizen, a first-hand report on more of the world than any of its leaders had seen, and prove as nothing else could that "there are no distant

179

points in the world any longer," and that what concerns people in the farthest place on earth "must concern us almost as much as the problems of the people of California concern the people of New York." He intended to demonstrate that it was indeed one world, a world grown small, "and if the world of which we dream is to be achieved, even in part, then the United Nations must become a common council, not only for the winning of the war but for the future welfare of mankind."

The whole thing started when three American newspaper correspondents stationed in Russia's wartime capital at Kuibyshev sent Willkie a telegram suggesting a good-will visit. Willkie had been wanting to visit other Allied countries since his return from England. He wrote to President Roosevelt and said he would like to go to Russia and also into the Middle East and China because he felt there was an urgent need to demonstrate that all Americans, regardless of politics, were united in the war and to start people everywhere thinking in terms of postwar cooperation.

President Roosevelt immediately agreed. "I think that for many reasons Mr. Willkie should take this trip," he said in a memorandum to General George Marshall, Chief of Staff. He sent Willkie an enthusiastic telegram that he was making the preliminary arrangements and, "I hope you can come to see me at your convenience so that we can have a good talk in regard to it and in regard to a lot of other things."

On August 7, following a White House luncheon to honor Queen Wilhelmina of the Netherlands, Willkie and the President talked most of the afternoon. The President then sent a message to Stalin, explaining that while Willkie had been his election opponent, "he is heart and soul with my administration in our foreign policy and is greatly helping with the war work," and that "for the sake of the present and the future I personally think that a visit to the Soviet Union

180

by Mr. Willkie would be a good thing." Stalin agreed, sent Willkie an invitation, and the trip became the front-page news that it was to remain for weeks to come.

Willkie returned to the White House two weeks later to work out detailed plans with the President and other top officials. During their conference, the President referred to him as "Private Citizen Number One" and later told reporters that Willkie would perform some "special tasks" as his personal representative and would deliver some personal messages for him to other world leaders. Willkie's mission in general, the President said, would be to tell the world the truth about America's war effort and to "compare what an Axis victory would mean as contrasted with a United Nations triumph." From the White House, Willkie went to the State Department for a briefing, conferred for two hours with Secretary of State Hull, and then had a talk with Russian Ambassador Maxim Litvinov.

He left New York's Mitchel Field on August 26, 1942 for the international take-off point at West Palm Beach, Florida, aboard a four-motored Army bomber converted to a transport plane and named the *Gulliver* after Jonathan Swift's fictional voyager. Aboard the plane, piloted by Major Richard Kight and with a six-man crew, were the close friends Willkie had chosen as his companions, publisher Gardner Cowles and foreign correspondent Joseph Barnes, both of whom were with the Office of War Information, Major Grant Mason of the Army, and Willkie's brother-in-law, his sister Charlotte's husband, Navy Captain Paul Pihl.

After a brief stop in Puerto Rico, where Willkie had a chance to see his son Philip, stationed there at a Navy base, the *Gulliver* touched down at Belém near the mouth of the Amazon and then at Natal for the flight across the South Atlantic to the secret American airfield at Ascension Island. By way of Accra on the African Gold Coast, Kano's fantastic walled city of mud huts in Northern Nigeria, and a night's stay in the fabled governor's palace in Khartoum in the Sudan, Willkie arrived in Cairo on August 31.

The first thing he asked American correspondents when he stepped from the plane was how the Dodgers were doing in the baseball pennant race back home. He stressed his role of the visiting private citizen by making a sightseeing tour of the Sphinx and the Pyramids, but he also had a conference with Egypt's Premier Nahas Pasha, an audience with King Farouk, and made sure the correspondents reported his more serious views that were intended to focus American attention on the Middle East and to inspire confidence in eventual Allied victory.

There were wild rumors at the time that Nazi General Rommel was about to drive the British completely out of Egypt. Willkie accepted an invitation from Field Marshal Montgomery to visit the front where the Allies were building up for the turning battle of El Alamein and under artillery fire he toured sections of the desert battle area, saw planes shot down, and climbed into wrecked Nazi tanks. The British commander frankly detailed his position and his strategy, and convinced Willkie that Rommel had been stopped and soon would be driven back. Montgomery couldn't say so, for reasons of strategy, but Willkie did. Together they called a press conference and in an announcement designed to strengthen Allied morale Willkie flatly declared: "Egypt is saved. Rommel is stopped and a beginning has been made on the task of throwing the Nazis out of Africa." Prime Minister Churchill later told Willkie that his statement "did no end of good" and that the ensuing battle confirmed "all your most sanguine forecasts."

Throughout the Middle East, he found backwardness, poverty, squalor, a need for more public health work, and

182

more education, but most of all the need for "social dignity and self-confidence which come from freedom and self-rule." Lacking a middle class, dominated by wealthy men who had little awareness of the people's needs, "the great mass are impoverished, own no property, are hideously ruled," he said. "One senses a ferment in these lands, a groping of the long-inert masses" for some way to achieve "their intense, almost fanatical aspirations," and unless democracy opened the doors to them they would turn to the hope communism seemed to offer or "to fervid nationalism." In the "lack of equilibrium between these peoples and their world" he saw "a potential source of conflict, the possible origin of another war."

He flew on to Ankara, the capital of then neutral Turkey, and when Axis propagandists protested to the Turkish government against his visit, Willkie said with wry humor that if the Nazis didn't like it they should ask the Turks to invite the leader of Hitler's opposition party in Germany to come for a visit. He turned up in a plain blue business suit among dinner-jacketed and uniformed guests to attend a banquet in his honor, and put a strain on the services of his Turkish interpreter as he stopped to talk to crowds in the streets, who were delighted when they finally understood the translation of such statements as, "If you want to see the United Nations win, don't just sit in the bleachers and throw pop bottles."

In Beirut, Lebanon, he met and tried to understand the complex personality of General Charles De Gaulle, then leader of the Fighting French Movement, to whom he talked for hours in the general's private room, "where every corner, every wall, held busts, statues and pictures of Napoleon." De Gaulle explained to Willkie that while he was "perfectly willing to sit with Winston Churchill and Franklin Roosevelt and consider ways and means by which French rights and French territories could be momentarily used" to drive the Nazis and the collaborators out of France, "—in no place in this world can I yield a single French right." People should keep "France's glorious history" in mind, De Gaulle told him, and not forget "that I and my associates represent France" and are "the legatees of all of France and its possessions."

The *Gulliver* took Willkie to Jerusalem, where he set up an interview room in the home of American consul Lowell Pinkerton, and arranged to talk alternately to Jewish and Arab leaders. They came in succession, up one staircase and out by means of another, so that throughout a long day and evening he was able to hear spokesmen from all factions of the troubled question of what to do about the future of Palestine. What was needed, he felt afterwards, as elsewhere in the world, was to break down ancient prejudices and differences among people. But he admitted "it is probably unrealistic to believe that such a complex question," involving religion, history, and high international politics, "can be solved by good will and simple honesty."

In Baghdad, Iraq, the royal band was at the airport and crowds lined the streets to welcome him as he was driven to dinner at the palace, but on the way, he impulsively stopped the car outside a native coffee shop, went in and unceremoniously straddled the nearest chair, ordered a cup of coffee, and kept royalty waiting while he talked to the people. He found the city something out of the *Arabian Nights*, with its mosques piercing gold minarets into the sky, and bazaars where copper and silver craftsmen worked as in ancient times, but in the stores he found "machine-made trinkets from New York," small symbols of the new world's thrust into the old.

At Teheran, the capital of Iran, the *Gulliver* picked up the

Soviet pilots assigned to it for the flight into Russia, and on Thursday, September 17, Willkie arrived in Kuibyshev, the temporary wartime capital on the Volga some five hundred miles southeast of Moscow.

Chapter Eighteen

WENDELL WILLKIE was up at sunrise his first morning in Russia to visit factories, farms, schools, and libraries and to talk to as many average Russian people as he could. He said the government had promised to let him come and go as freely as he would in the United States and to let him ask questions "without limit or interference," and he lost no time in taking the Russians up on that promise.

He admired the cows at a collective farm, but had a friendly debate with the farm manager over collective ownership, toured an enormous aircraft factory that had been moved back in sections from near the fighting front, and had a debate with the plant engineer over factory production under communism. He took over the wheel of a boat himself to steer it part way up the Volga to visit a huge power development project. Attending the ballet, he won over the audience by jumping from his box to the stage at the finish of the performance to present a bouquet to the prima ballerina. He kissed her cheek and the audience shouted, "Weel-ki!"

After a dinner given in his honor by Deputy Foreign

Minister Andrei Vishinsky his last night in Kuibyshev, Willkie went on to Moscow, where a crowd turned out to greet him despite pouring rain. Monday morning he took off on his own with two reporters for an after-breakfast walk through the city, then visited more factories and attended an evening performance at the Moscow Symphony. The next day he went through a munitions plant, toured Moscow's antiaircraft defenses, attended an American embassy reception in his honor, and went to a jazz concert.

He and Stalin talked for three hours at the Kremlin on Wednesday evening. Willkie personally delivered the messages that had been entrusted to him by President Roosevelt, and Stalin gave him some information to take back to the President that was too secret to be trusted to coded messages or even to regular diplomatic channels. Their conversation touched on many things: the war and what would come after, American production methods which Stalin greatly admired, Willkie's estimate of the efficiency of various Russian factories he had visited and about which Stalin asked searching and detailed questions, and Soviet schools and libraries. Willkie told Stalin the schools he had seen seemed to be good ones, but added as a joke, "If you continue to educate the Russian people, Mr. Stalin, the first thing you know you'll educate yourself out of a job." Stalin threw back his head and roared with laughter.

Willkie was surprised to find him a much shorter and more stockily-built man than he had expected, and also was somewhat startled by Stalin's pink tunic and pastel blue trousers. Although Stalin spoke quietly and simply, he impressed Willkie as having a hard, tenacious, driving mind, and as being a man who was impatient with generalities, pleasantries, and compliments. "He is a hard man, perhaps even a cruel man, but a very able one," Willkie said later. "He has few illusions."

187

Russia's military situation was then desperate, and Stalin frankly told Willkie so. He spoke eloquently of the struggle to defend Stalingrad but wouldn't predict that Russia could hold it. Dramatically, he talked of the need for fuel, transportation, military equipment, and manpower; he admitted a deep suspicion that some of the Allies were deliberately delaying the opening of a second front in Europe, complained that Russia was bearing the main force of Nazi assault, and that the Allies were not doing enough to help.

At midnight, after his visit to the Kremlin, Willkie climbed into a jeep for a secrecy-shrouded visit to the Russian fighting front. He rode through the night in a cold rain and arrived after nine in the morning at the headquarters of the Rzhev sector. When Willkie asked General Lelushenko how large an area he was defending, the General answered, "I'm not defending anything—I'm attacking." Without stopping to eat, they drove to within a few miles of the front lines where Willkie walked through debris on the battlefield while shells burst far overhead. After dinner with the General he returned to Moscow.

Willkie issued a statement to the press the next day that made sensational news. "I am now convinced that we can best help by establishing a real second front in Western Europe at the earliest possible moment our military leaders will approve," he said. "And perhaps some of them will need some public prodding. Next summer might be too late."

Unknown to Willkie, the Allied command already had decided to establish a second front in North Africa rather than on the European continent because the Allies were not yet prepared for a full-scale invasion of Europe. Willkie's statement, planned to improve relations with Russia and to force public discussion of the problem, drew some angry comments from Washington and London. Even President Roosevelt, who had not kept Willkie informed of the North

Africa decision, seemed briefly annoyed. But the President dismissed the matter as "speculative" and told reporters Willkie was carrying out his mission "extremely well." If Willkie had aroused a furor, he also had helped temporarily to ease Russians' suspicions of America and Britain.

Willkie had another chance to talk to Stalin before he left Moscow when he sat next to him for some five hours through the numerous courses of a state dinner the Russian premier gave for him. Afterwards Willkie told reporters: "You may agree with him or disagree with him, condemn or praise the Russian social system, but don't discount his abilities or his purposes." He was greatly impressed by the Russian people, but depressed by communist control over them, and especially by its destruction of individual freedoms. Yet he was convinced that Russia was "a dynamic country and a force that cannot be bypassed in any future world."

From Moscow, he flew to Tashkent in Uzbek, then over the Asian desert and also some of the highest mountain ranges in the world, through the back door into China, to Tihwa, the capital of the vast western province of Sinkiang, to Lanchow on the Yellow River, south to Chengtu, and finally to Chungking. All along the route, he stopped to visit factories, schools, military installations and training centers, and to talk to the leaders and the people. He was greeted by crowds that lined roads for miles, and was feted at so many ceremonial banquets that he remarked, "There is more danger of my being killed by the kindness of the Chinese than by enemy bullets." When the presence of Japanese planes delayed his flight from Chengtu, he said he felt "very much complimented" by the attention the enemy was giving him.

"I was conscious every day I was in China of the fact that China had been at war for five long years," he said. But beyond the war itself, everyone to whom he talked made

189

him deeply aware of "the revolution of ideas that is sweeping the East—a subject that came up wherever I went, of the overpowering surge toward freedom of Asia's hundreds of millions, of their demands for education and better living and, above all, for the right to their own governments, independent of the West."

He spent hours in the company of Generalissimo Chiang Kai-shek and with Madame Chiang, who, at Willkie's urging, later flew to the United States to tell China's story to the American people. Accompanied on other interviews by General Joseph Stilwell, commander of the China-Burma-India theater of war, he went with Stilwell to the headquarters of General Claire Chennault, the former Texas high school teacher and military aviation pioneer who had organized the American volunteer group of "Flying Tiger" pilots to fight the Japanese in China before the United States was in the war.

Willkie talked to Madame Sun, widow of Sun Yat-sen, founder of the Chinese Republic, and had a long discussion with Chinese communist leader Chou En-lai, then editing a newspaper in Chungking. General Chou had led communist forces against Chiang Kai-shek in the civil wars but was temporarily united with him in China's war against Japan. He impressed Willkie as being a very serious man of obvious ability, impatient over the slowness of reforms, willing to compromise for the sake of the war, but frankly unwilling to predict that Chinese unity would last when war ended.

Hearing and seeing at every turn the ferment of the people, in which there was "enough explosive powder in Central Asia to blow the lid off the world again when the present fighting is over," Willkie was more firmly than ever convinced that America had to make clear its determination, while the war was still under way, "to help the colonial people who join the United Nations' cause to become free

190

and independent nations." To those who argued that such questions should be hushed until victory was won, Willkie answered that "exactly the reverse is true," and that "sincere efforts to find progressive solutions now will strengthen our cause." He said: "Opponents of social change always urge delay because of some present crisis. After the war, changes may be too little and too late."

So, upon leaving Chungking, he issued a statement boldly intended to waken the world to the realization of the revolution he feared surely would explode in China and throughout the East unless something definite was done to end Western colonialism. He knew it would cause more of an uproar among the Allies than anything he had said during his entire trip, and that was exactly what he hoped it would do.

Believing that the war involved far more than merely winning battles, that it was "a war to win men's minds," and that "mankind is on the march and the old colonial times are past," he said that while the people of Asia, who had never known democracy, "may or may not want our type of democracy, they are determined to work out their own destiny under governments selected by themselves." Bluntly, Willkie declared: "We believe this war must mean an end to the empire of nations over other nations. No foot of Chinese soil should be or can be ruled from now on except by the people who live on it."

Back home there were violent denunciations of him in Congress, attacks in the press, a renewed outcry from his old isolationist enemies, the chilled reaction of Wall Street financial circles, even disapproval from some of his own friends. To the British, Willkie's statement seemed to strike not only at the entire colonial empire around the world but specifically at Hong Kong and at India. Prime Minister Churchill himself answered: "We mean to hold our own. I did not become the King's First Minister to preside over the liquidation of the British Empire."

Willkie had known the criticism would come, but with it came public discussion. He also knew that President Roosevelt, no admirer of colonialism, had to consider the vital wartime need for British friendship, and couldn't support any call upon Britain and the other Allies to give up their colonies to the people who lived in them. Willkie once again had taken a position beyond that which the President could take. He was annoyed when he was told that the President had joined in mildly criticizing him. But he made it clear in Chungking that he was not speaking for the President. "When I speak for myself," he told reporters, "I'm Wendell Willkie and I say what I damn please."

One small but immediate result was an announcement by the State Department, after some eight years of promises and delays, that the United States and Britain were ready to begin final negotiations to give up extraterritorial rights that had kept Chinese courts from jurisdiction over American and British companies and citizens in China.

Willkie meanwhile went on from Chungking to visit his third fighting front of the war along the Yellow River beyond Sian. Proceeding by train, handcar, and then on foot, he reached a position close enough to look through a telescope across the river into the muzzles of Japanese guns, while the Chinese line was attacked by artillery fire and by twenty-three Japanese bombers that destroyed one of the railroad coaches.

The *Gulliver* began its return journey on October 9, taking off from Chengtu at dawn for a 1600-mile flight across northern China, over the Gobi Desert and Mongolia to Chita in Siberia, and from there, on a thousand-mile leap to the Soviet Republic of Yakutsk, close to the Arctic Circle.

While weather delayed the plane there, Willkie had a chance to tour the small capital city, which he found to be booming in a way that reminded him of Elwood in his youth. New industries were flourishing in the one-time Czarist penal colony, there was a busy trade in gold and furs, and a young communist official boasted of the future of the place "like a California real estate salesman." In that bustling far outpost of Soviet civilization he found a theater, concert and cultural groups, a fine museum, and a library stocked with 550,000 volumes.

From the frozen little village of Seincham, the *Gulliver* made the first eastward American flight of the war over the Bering Strait to Fairbanks, Alaska. After a stop at Edmonton, Alberta, and another at Minneapolis, it carried Willkie toward the final and first really dangerous landing of the entire journey, in a heavy rainstorm at Washington's National Airport on October 14. Ten pounds lighter than when he had left, shaggy-haired from lack of a haircut, he waved jovially to reporters and the waiting crowd, stepped before the radio microphones and newsreel cameras, and said, "I'm damned glad to be home."

Three-quarters of an hour later he arrived at the White House to make his report to President Roosevelt. He delivered his confidential messages, relayed the information gained from his interviews with the leaders of various nations, and then talked to the President for an hour and a half about the disturbing conditions he had found. Reportedly he used extremely frank language in advising the President that America should not commit itself indefinitely to supporting imperialism and colonialism but should declare to the peoples of Africa, the Middle East, and Asia that the United States was determined to help them establish political freedom and economic liberty. They finished their conference in a genial and understanding mood and after the President had thanked him, Willkie held a press interview in the White House lobby.

He spent the night in New York and the next day went to Rushville where Mrs. Willkie and Philip, who was home on a brief leave from the Navy, were waiting for him to join them. There he managed to get a little rest and relaxation visiting his farms, but he also worked on the text of the nationwide broadcast he intended to make as a "Report to the People." Delivered over all four networks on the night of October 26, it was heard by a then-record audience of thirty-six million listeners. Many considered it Willkie's greatest speech.

The world had become small, he said, not only in terms of air travel which had brought "the myriad millions of the Far East as close to us as Los Angeles is to New York by fast train," but because the peoples of the world had been brought close to each other in ideas, and in such a world military victory was less important than what followed it. "We must plan now for peace on a global basis," he said. "The world must be free, economically and politically, for nations and for men so that peace may exist in it. America must play an active and constructive part in freeing it and keeping its peace." Willkie went on:

Men and women all over the world are on the march, physically, intellectually and spiritually. After centuries of ignorance and dull compliance, hundreds of millions of people in Eastern Europe and Asia have opened the books. Old fears no longer frighten them. They are no longer willing to be Eastern slaves for Western profits. The big house on the hill surrounded by mud huts has lost its awesome charm.

Our Western World and our presumed supremacy are now on trial. Our boasting and our big talk leave Asia cold. Men and women in Russia and China and in the Middle East are conscious now of their own potential strength. They are coming to know that many of the decisions about the future of the world lie in their hands. And they intend that these decisions shall leave the peoples of each nation free from foreign domination, free for economic, social and spiritual growth.

Many of them, he said, still hoped America would join them "as one of their partners" in helping to create a new society of world cooperation, "free alike of the economic injustices of the West and the political malpractices of the East." But, he said, as partners, "they want us neither hesitant, incompetent nor afraid. They want a partner who will not hesitate to speak out against injustice anywhere in the world."

Chapter Nineteen

"THIS is a war for freedom—freedom here and freedom elsewhere," Wendell Willkie said. "But freedom is of the mind." There was no military force on earth that alone could bring the war to real victory, he argued, and no agreements between nations that could automatically produce a better world. "The final victory," he repeated, "will be won on the battlefields of men's minds."

In a speech at Duke University, he urged: "Spread the facts, analyze them, make them available to all the world. There is no other form of warfare that can possibly win the great political struggle in which we are engaged. Truth alone can win it." Again, in a radio broadcast, he declared that "our leaders must be constantly exposed to democracy's greatest driving power—the whiplash of public opinion, developed from honest, free discussion." And in an article written for the *London Evening Standard* he said, "I have been deliberately trying to provoke and, if you will, to 'prod' the leaders . . . into frank statements of their postwar purposes."

He was still the challenger. In this great debate over the

aims of war and peace, as in every other debate of his life, he was deliberately trying to provoke argument, to get people to think, to speak out, to differ with him if they pleased, but to realize that much of the world was in revolution against the ways of the past. If some of his ideas were visionary and the goals seemed almost impossible to achieve, that too was part of his challenge.

Determined to reach as many people as he could in every way that he could, he spoke at public forums, to colleges, labor and business groups, gave off-the-record talks to reporters, wrote articles and made radio broadcasts. "Every one of us has the obligation to speak out, to exchange ideas freely and frankly, across the Pacific, across the Atlantic, here at home," he said at a *New York Herald Tribune* Forum. "For unless people know what we are thinking here in America and unless we have a similar idea of what they are thinking . . . there can be no agreement. We must know what they aim for and we must let them know our aims."

He argued that this should not be limited to the nations that were formal allies in the war. "We must try to find out and openly express the desires and hopes of hundreds of millions of other peoples—in the torn heart of Europe, in India, on the embattled shores of the Mediterranean, in Africa, on the southern shores of Asia, and in our own hemisphere," he said. And world cooperation would have to produce more than political agreements and the exchange of "pretty talk" among nations, he told an audience in Toronto. Any future world organization that hoped to succeed would have to deal in "practical realities," he said, and develop "economic and social plans to raise standards of living," and work toward "the elimination of trade barriers and a more equitable distribution of raw materials."

He had never written a book, despite his literary interests,

197

but he turned now to writing one in which he could expand his "Report to the People." He made use of the notes and recollections of his traveling companions, Joseph Barnes and Gardner Cowles, and had the editorial advice of Irita Van Doren, but the writing was his. For weeks, on a regular nine-to-twelve schedule, he devoted his mornings to it, working to the point where "every time I think of having to write something more I get nauseated."

Sometimes he would sit sucking the end of a pencil, thinking out his ideas to scribble on a pad, and at other times he would pace the room dictating to a typist. His rough copy was triple-spaced so he had plenty of room to make changes and corrections. Second drafts were heavily black-penciled, and even after the book was in type he made hundreds of changes in the galley proofs to strike out words that seemed too emotional and to phrase passages exactly as he wanted them. "I write entirely with a purpose," he told an interviewer. "I pretend no literary skill. I write what I think and then rewrite."

The book's original title was *One War, One Peace, One World,* but his publishers suggested changing it simply to *One World.* It was published on April 8, 1943, and within four days after publication 170,000 copies had been sold. Before the end of the year three million copies of various editions had been printed, it had topped the best-seller list for twenty-one weeks, was being translated into nearly every foreign language, and bootleg editions were being distributed to the underground in countries under Nazi rule. Willkie established a trust fund to receive all income from it and to donate the money to various societies and public institutions.

Written in a clear and simple style, it told entertainingly of his world adventures, but also explained his belief that all peoples, regardless of race, language, religion or nationality had certain needs in common, to which individual freedom and the right of self-government were basic, and that these rights had to be guaranteed by world cooperation if there ever was to be lasting peace. Read by millions around the world and especially in America, it had the effect on public opinion he was seeking, and its reception pleased him more than anything else in his life. "My life has been unbelievably full of satisfaction," he told a meeting of the Council on Books in Wartime, "but this was the richest satisfaction of all."

But if there was to be understanding among the peoples of the world, Willkie believed, it must start at home with a firm insistence upon equal rights and civil liberties for all Americans. "We cannot fight the forces and ideas of imperialism abroad and maintain a form of imperialism at home," he said at a Los Angeles conference of the National Association for the Advancement of Colored People. "The defense of our democracy against the forces that threaten it from without has made some of its failures to function at home glaringly apparent. . . . When we talk of freedom and opportunity for all nations the increasing paradoxes in our own society become so clear they can no longer be ignored."

Minority groups—racial, political, or otherwise—provide democracy with the "constant spring of new ideas, stimulating new thought and action, the constant source of new vigor," he wrote in an article in *The Saturday Evening Post*, "and to suppress minority thinking and minority expression would tend to freeze society and prevent progress" because "the majority itself is stimulated by the existence of minority groups" and the "human mind requires contrary expressions against which to test itself."

But, he warned in another statement, "We are living once more in a period that is psychologically susceptible to witch-hunting and mob-baiting." Denouncing the "excessive activity of the investigating bureaus of Congress and the Administration, with their indecent searching out of private lives," he said: "Each of us, if not alert, may find himself the unconscious carrier of the germ that will destroy our freedom. For each of us has within himself the inheritance of age-long hatreds, of racial and religious differences, and everyone has a tendency to find the cause for his own failures in some imagined conspiracy of evil."

He made a decision his friends warned him would be "political suicide" when he agreed to appear before the Supreme Court to defend the right to citizenship of an admitted former Communist. Some of his enemies declared it marked his "final capture" by the "forces of internationalism, liberalism and the Kremlin," and some of his old opponents within the Republican party charged that he favored "Reds over Republicans." Willkie said, "I could not, with my beliefs, have remained satisfied with myself if I refused to accept the case."

It involved William Schneiderman, whose naturalized citizenship the Department of Justice was trying to revoke on the grounds that he had been a Communist at the time he applied to become a citizen in 1927. Willkie submitted his brief to the Supreme Court in January, 1942, and appeared before the Court in November, armed with only "a much tracked-up record, a sheaf of quotations, and a page of notes scrawled in pencil."

His informal extemporaneous argument, salted with occasional wisecracks that produced laughter from the justices, somewhat shook the traditional solemnity of the court, but he too was solemn as he argued that a decision against Schneiderman would set up a double standard for citizenship, one standard for those who were native-born and another for those who had been naturalized. Willkie said that while he held no brief for Communism, and that if

200

Schneiderman could understand its confusing theories "he's a better man than I am," it was unfair to deport him because of the social views he had held fifteen years before, or to condemn him for exercising freedom of thought and of speech when he had never been questioned about his beliefs at the time he first applied for citizenship.

He appeared to present further arguments in February, and in June the Supreme Court ruled in Schneiderman's favor, holding there was no proof that Schneiderman personally accepted the views of some Communists who advocated violent overthrow of the government. Justice Rutledge, in his opinion, said that if Schneiderman's citizenship could be revoked after so many years, the same thing could be done "after thirty or fifty years" to "tens of thousands of others" who were naturalized citizens. Willkie hailed the decision as one which had kept the government from establishing "a thoroughly illiberal precedent." Years later, the Court changed its position under the provisions of the Smith Act, but later still that was questioned and the issue remained in controversy. Willkie's victory stood for a time, encouraged free speech, and helped ease relations with Russia during the period when the United Nations organization was to be born.

When he was honored with an award by the National Conference of Christians and Jews, he said: "In the courtroom and from the public rostrum, I will fight for the preservation of civil liberties, no matter how unpopular the cause may be in any given instance." And when he accepted the American Hebrew Medal for 1942, he objected to the word "tolerance" in the official citation that went with it. "It is not 'tolerance' that anyone is entitled to in America," he said. "It is the right of every citizen in America to be treated by other citizens as an equal. No man has the right in America to treat any other man 'tolerantly,' for 'tolerance' is the assumption of superiority. Our liberties are the equal rights of all."

He was named a member of the Committee on the Bill of Rights of the American Bar Association, was a frequent speaker on behalf of minorities in Voice of America broadcasts to Europe, an early supporter of the Emergency Committee to Save the Jewish People of Europe, a broad member of the National Urban League, and a trustee of the large Negro college, Hampton Institute. In the spring of 1942, he played a large part in the campaign to open Navy and Marine Corps ranks to Negro volunteers. As a motion picture executive, he took Negro leaders with him on trips to Hollywood for conferences with producers, directors, and others in the film industry, to demand an end to the stereotype presentation of the Negro as a clown or a servant in movies.

The worst race riots of the war years, in Detroit in June, 1943, when thirty-four persons were killed and seven hundred injured, gave terrible emphasis to his demand for "practical, direct and positive action" instead of "empty talk" to secure for Negroes their rights as citizens and human beings. That meant, he said, not only "adequate and decent housing," but also "legal equality, equal opportunity for education, economic equality, and equality of expenditure of public money for health and hospitalization." Invited to present a postscript to a nationwide broadcast called an *Open Letter to the American People*, Willkie accused both major political parties of failing to satisfy even "the least human needs" of Negroes. He said:

> One party has the tendency to ask the Negro for his vote as a recompense for a simple act of justice done eighty years ago. The other retains political power by, in effect, depriving the Negro of his right to vote in one part of the country while seeking his vote in another on the plea of great friendship for his race. One party cannot go on feeling that it has no further obli-

gation to the Negro citizen because Abraham Lincoln freed the slaves. And the other party is not entitled to power if it sanctions and practices one set of principles in Atlanta and another in Harlem.

This was not just a domestic problem, he maintained. America's standing in the world was at stake. He went on:

Two-thirds of the people who are allied with us do not have white skins. Today the white man is professing friendship and a desire to cooperate and is promising opportunity in the world to come when the war is over. They wonder. When the necessities of war cease to make cooperation valuable to the white man, will his promises mean anything? Race riots do not reassure them.

The United Nations began as only a phrase, coined by President Roosevelt, to describe the nations at war against the Axis powers. It gradually came into use simply to mean "the Allies." The first official use of it was in December, 1942 when twenty-six nations joined in a Declaration of the United Nations to continue their joint war efforts and not to seek a separate peace. But it still was used to describe only unity in war, and what Willkie urged in dozens of speeches and articles—as he had in his book—was a firm commitment by the United Nations to establish a postwar world organization. As the tide of war slowly began to turn in Allied favor early in 1943, he saw the need as more pressing than ever before so there would be no American retreat to the isolation that had wrecked the League of Nations after the First World War.

"We will have no United Nations after the war," he warned in a radio broadcast, "unless we make the United Nations now a fact and not a mere euphonious phrase. Successful instruments of international government cannot be created in a day." In another broadcast on the Fourth of

July, he called upon his countrymen to recognize that "the world is one world, that all parts of it for their own well-being are interdependent," and said that the immediate need was not to celebrate the Declaration of Independence but for "a declaration of interdependence among the nations of this one world."

Many other voices had joined his in urging the nation to begin planning for the peace that was to come, even though months of war still had to be fought. Under Secretary of State, Sumner Welles, called for "the United Nations to draw up a postwar program now for policing the world against new aggression." Minnesota's Harold Stassen proposed a "World Parliament." And in Congress, resolutions to create various kinds of committees to study preparations for peace were offered by both Democrats and Republicans. Even some formerly strong isolationists, such as Senator Taft, expressed willingness to consider something "along the general lines suggested in the League of Nations."

Willkie threw his full influence behind a resolution introduced in mid-March, 1943, by two Republican senators, Ball of Minnesota and Burton of Ohio, and two Democrats, Hatch of New Mexico and Hill of Alabama. It provided for "the establishment of procedures and machinery for the settlement of peacetime disputes and disagreements among nations and for the assembly and maintenance of a United Nations' military force available for immediate use against any future attempt at military aggression by any nation." There were amendments and substitute resolutions offered, one by Michigan's Senator Arthur Vandenberg, who was changing his isolationist views and soon would take the historic step of becoming spokesman for a bipartisan foreign policy based on world cooperation.

The United Nations organization for which Willkie had fought so long finally became a definite promise in October,

1943 when the Big Three Foreign Ministers, meeting in Moscow, issued a statement that recognized "the necessity of establishing at the earliest practicable date a general international organization based on the principle of the sovereign equality of all peace-loving states," with membership open to all such states "large and small, for the maintenance of peace and security." The United States Senate, after its long delay, finally passed a modified resolution in November, approving the statement of the Foreign Ministers and declaring that "the United States, acting through its Constitutional processes, join with free and sovereign nations in the establishment and maintenance of international authority with power to prevent aggression and maintain the peace of the world."

It was far from what Willkie wanted. He went on battling without success the rest of his life for the establishment of a United Nations Council while the war was still underway, so that its aims and its set-up would be firmly in operation before the war ended. Also without success, he continued to fight to provide the United Nations with "the machinery needed to enforce its decisions" so that it would not become a "mere debating society." But at least he saw his basic idea of a world body of nations on its way to realization, and knew that he had greatly helped to create the public opinion and the political acceptance which made the United Nations possible. His "loyal opposition" of 1940 helped pave the way for bipartisan foreign policy, and his stand within the Republican party helped to turn it from isolation toward the views necessary to obtain American approval of the United Nations Charter.

But Wendell Willkie had made himself truly a man without a party. As the nation approached a new presidential election in 1944, he had far more enemies than friends among Republican politicians. From the moment of his nomination in 1940, some party professionals had regarded him as a "Democrat" who had tried to capture the party and make it over in his own image; and everything he had done since, in fighting for the things in which he believed at the cost of party harmony, had alienated or enraged powerful Republicans.

He had put principles above practical politics, had failed to provide leadership that would unify the party through compromise, and had considered the party an "instrument" through which he could bring about the changes he believed vital. The party bosses were determined to get rid of him, to kill him politically once and for all, and to put a definite stop to any attempt he might make to regain the nomination in 1944.

It became obvious by early 1943 that Willkie wanted another chance at the presidency, to put into effect the policies for which he had fought, but he still would not compromise. His position was that only a fully liberal Republican party would have a chance of winning the election and that the party would have to take him on his own terms or risk defeat in November. But he had little power to back his stand, and he underestimated the determination of his opponents. He felt he had a gambling chance to capture the nomination again with a sweep of popular support, to repeat what had happened at the 1940 convention, by carrying his appeal over the heads of the party professionals directly to Republican voters.

His opponents had not decided on the man they meant to put against Willkie. New York's Governor Thomas E. Dewey seemed the most likely choice, the leader in all Republican popularity polls, but Dewey's public stand was that he was not a candidate. During the summer of 1943, Willkie went to Rushville for what was supposed to be a vacation but he spent most of his time talking to the few party leaders who still supported him.

He made a trip through the Midwestern states, talking to Republican groups—from precinct leaders up—and sounding them out, and he followed that with other trips that covered a good part of the country, to talk in person to as many Republicans as he could. In great swings to Colorado, Missouri, Wisconsin and back, to Louisiana, Texas, and other states, he shook hands, made speeches, held closed-door meetings and public rallies. With the national committee and most leaders against him, he tried to improvise his own political organization.

Willkie still had a large popular following and his actual political strength with party voters was unknown, so Republican leaders couldn't openly disown him. But they shut him out of party councils, conferences, and high-level meetings and issued party statements and resolutions that pointedly ignored him. They maneuvered to embarrass him and put him on the defensive. Widely-publicized questionnaires, issued in the name of one party faction or another, asked such loaded questions as whether he wanted to put American armed forces "under the control of a world state," and whether he favored "flooding the country with alien individuals and alien ideas."

Prodded beyond endurance by one such group, Willkie told them, "I don't know whether you're going to support me and I don't give a damn. You're a bunch of political liabilities anyhow." He went on to add that he was not accountable to them for what he thought, "or to anybody else except the people." But to get support and to raise the funds to carry on his campaign he had to prove he had a following among the party's voters. He couldn't avoid the primary elections as he had in 1940. He was forced to test his popularity. If he meant to run again, he had to show some strength against the party machine and the primaries were his only way of doing that.

He was unable to choose some states in which he would have preferred to run, and where he could count on making good showings, because "favorite sons" had announced themselves as primary candidates, men with strong local followings he couldn't hope to beat. Finally, he had little choice but to make his first real test in Wisconsin, where he had done fairly well in 1940 but where isolationist feelings were strong. He announced that he would run in New Hampshire on March 14, Wisconsin on April 4, and then in Nebraska and Oregon.

Willkie launched his national campaign in New York, and early in February, 1944 left on a speaking trip which took him across the country and back, touching the states he hadn't visited earlier so that within a year he had spoken in all but four of the forty-eight states. He arrived in New Hampshire on March 10, for one major address there before the primary. When the vote was taken four days later, Willkie had captured six of New Hampshire's eleven delegates to the Republican National Convention, Dewey had won two, and three others were unpledged. It was a victory, but disappointing because he had expected to do much better.

He arrived in Madison, Wisconsin, on March 18 and made forty speeches in thirteen days, alternately denouncing the Democrats and the Old Guard of the Republican party from one end of the state to the other. None of the other primary candidates went to Wisconsin or even admitted they were candidates; but behind the scenes, the party politicians were hard at work against Willkie. Large sums of money were poured into the campaign in which all other candidates pretended not to be running.

Nearly exhausted by his Wisconsin tour, he went on to Nebraska after one day's rest to start campaigning for the next primary there while awaiting the returns from Wisconsin. Behind him in Wisconsin, the Dewey forces sprang into action by plastering the state with billboards and posters, making around-the-clock radio announcements, and mailing thousands of circulars, so their drive would have its strongest impact after Willkie had left. Joking with reporters, Willkie offered to bet against himself, but most newspapers were predicting he would win a majority of Wisconsin's delegates.

He had planned an eleven-day speaking tour of Nebraska. He had made three speeches there and was in a hotel room at Norfolk, Nebraska, at midnight on April 4, when he heard the news from Wisconsin. Dewey had won seventeen delegates, Stassen four, General Douglas McArthur three. Willkie had won none.

The next day he went on to keep previously scheduled speaking engagements at West Point and Fremont, and then to Omaha where a crowd of three thousand awaited him. After a formal speech on foreign policy, he put aside his prepared text, changed his tone and quietly told his listeners:

I wish I could speak to you from my heart tonight. I cannot because there are too many factors that prevent it. If I spoke what's on my mind, I would make too great a castigation of American politics.

I had been encouraged to believe that the Republican party could live up to the standards of its founders, but I am discouraged to believe that it may be the party of negation. It is apparent that the average citizen fails to realize the far-reaching effect upon him of what is going on in the rest of the world or to realize that a war anywhere has its effect upon him. . . . I want the Republican party to be the leader, not

209

the follower, in cooperation with other nations so that the fires of war can be restrained. . . . Perhaps the conscience of America is dulled. Perhaps the people are not willing to bear the sacrifices, and I feel a sense of sickening because I know how much my party could do to make it worthy of its traditions.

And then he read the brief formal statement he had been working on all day. He was withdrawing from the presidential race and canceling the rest of his campaign. "It is obvious now that I cannot be nominated," he said. "Therefore I am asking my friends to desist from any activity toward that end and not to present my name at the convention."

He took the train back to New York that night, relaxed by playing Gin Rummy awhile and then by reading from one of his favorite novels, *The Count of Monte Cristo,* and when reporters pressed him about his future plans he smiled a little wearily and said, "I'm going to put about four hundred acres of my farms into corn."

Chapter Twenty

WENDELL WILLKIE would never become President of the United States. The ambition was now gone. But the possibilities that lay ahead of him in the spring of 1944 left him anything but a gloomy and beaten man. "It was a good fight," he wrote a friend, "but there are many battles yet ahead." In another letter he said, "I know that most people assume that one situated as I am must be depressed. As a matter of fact, I am on top of the wave."

He and President Roosevelt were considering a plan that neither of them could yet talk about openly, the possibility that they might combine their political influence to bring about a fundamental change in the traditional party system by creating between them a new liberal party in the United States. But that was in the future, and more immediate was the coming election of 1944, in which President Roosevelt would seek a fourth term, with the likelihood that Thomas E. Dewey would be his Republican opponent.

"I happen to believe that this is the most critical moment in the history of liberty," Willkie wrote in a personal off-the-record letter to some twenty newspaper editors and columnists who were his friends. "All I personally believe in is at stake—free government, civil liberty, economic justice and real accord, not alone among the nations, but among the peoples of the world. . . . I am going to do my duty at this time as my conscience permits me to see my duty, no matter what the price in criticism. . . . Naturally, as a Republican, I would prefer to work within the Republican party, but I will not sit by while the peace of the world is wrecked as it was in the 20's."

He would have no voice in the Republican National Convention's choice of a presidential candidate or in the platform it adopted. But even after his defeat in the Wisconsin primary, he still had a personal following of thousands of American voters and Republican leaders who took it for granted that he would automatically support the party and Dewey as its candidates, no matter what they stood for. They soon learned they were mistaken. Unless Dewey and the party went far to affirm the liberal international and domestic policies in which Willkie believed, he had no intention of announcing his support. He might remain silent. He might come out against Dewey. He might even bolt the party and throw his support to President Roosevelt.

Willkie honestly hadn't decided what to do, and his strategy was to leave his decision in doubt while he waited for Dewey and the Republican party to make their positions clearer. Meanwhile, the Democrats who hoped he might come over to their side also had to pay some attention to his views. So, to the extent of whatever influence various politicians believed he still had with the voters, he kept both parties courting his approval. In the end, his decision still remained in doubt and left politicians forever guessing as to what he might have done.

He pointedly stayed away from the Republican National

Convention that opened in Chicago on June 26. The work of the committee that was drafting the foreign relations plank was kept closely secret, but Willkie managed to get a copy of it. He called a news conference, made it public, and matched its wording to the foreign relations plank Republicans had adopted in 1920, when President Harding immediately after his election had announced that the League of Nations was a dead issue.

"A Republican president elected under the proposed platform of 1944 could with equal integrity announce that the United States would not enter any world organization in which the nations agreed jointly to use their 'sovereign' power for the suppression of aggression," Willkie charged. "The net result would be no international organization." He accused the party of failing to use its leadership and said, "We should speak in words forthright, clear and strong."

Republican leaders immediately denied that the platform could be used to repeat American refusal to join an international organization as in 1920, but Willkie had forced them to reaffirm their support of such an organization. When Dewey was nominated by the convention as expected, Willkie telegraphed his congratulations as a matter of "common courtesy," but newspapers noted that he carefully refrained from promising Dewey his support and, instead, congratulated him on having "one of the great opportunities of history for real leadership."

Many of Willkie's friends in the Republican Party were pressing him hard to come out for Dewey. Meanwhile, the pressure also was increasing from the Democratic side. Some important Democrats suggested that he should become President Roosevelt's running mate as the Democratic vice-presidential candidate. In the time between the Republican convention in June and the Democratic convention in July,

213

the rumors grew. According to President Roosevelt's correspondence, "feelers were put out" to Willkie early in July, and some sort of an offer was made to him, but apparently more to sound out his views than anything else.

President Roosevelt's first choice all along was Senator Harry Truman, who eventually won the nomination, and while some of the President's aides talked of Willkie as a possible vice-presidential candidate, Roosevelt himself probably never took the talk seriously, any more than Willkie did. But the rumors, along with others that Willkie might be offered a Cabinet post in the Roosevelt administration or that he might run for the Senate, helped keep politicians in doubt as to what he would do.

Dewey finally made a personal bid for Willkie's support by inviting him to come to the Governor's office in Albany to discuss what stand the Republican party should take on the conferences about to begin at the Dumbarton Oaks mansion in suburban Washington, to lay the groundwork for the United Nations organization. Willkie refused the invitation but said he would be willing to have Dewey's representative to the conference, John Foster Dulles, come and talk to him. He and Dulles met in New York, and discussed Willkie's views for an hour and a half. But again, Willkie had made it clear that he still had not decided whether to support Dewey. Willkie told friends the "period of watchful waiting" would continue for a time.

While all the immediate campaign maneuvering was going on, Willkie and President Roosevelt were looking beyond the 1944 election toward the possibility of working together to group all liberals somehow into one political party.

In various talks since 1940, they had discussed the "reactionaries" of both parties who stood in the way of liberal international and domestic programs. Roosevelt had fought

214

them in the Democratic party and Willkie had fought them in the Republican party and both had come to think of the problem along the same general lines. The two men had not talked together in person since Willkie's visit to the White House immediately after his world trip, but they began to exchange views through intermediaries and in letters, both of them cautious because of the political campaigns under way, yet looking toward a post-election alliance that might revolutionize politics in the United States.

The story didn't become public until long afterwards, but according to all accounts, the plan originated with Willkie. Apparently, after his primary election defeat and the failure of the Republican convention to adopt a platform he considered truly liberal, Willkie had become convinced that his party was completely in the control of conservatives, so he proposed uniting the liberal wings of the two great political parties and ridding them both of conservatives who then could group as they pleased.

President Roosevelt, according to his close associate Samuel Rosenman, was enthusiastic and said that if they went to work on it right after the election they might be able to bring about the change before 1948. He asked Rosenman to see Willkie, and Rosenman long afterward revealed that he held a two-hour meeting with Willkie at the St. Regis hotel in New York on July 5, which was kept secret to avoid any effect it might have on the election. Rosenman, by his own account, told Willkie that Roosevelt wanted to team up with him whether or not he was reelected in November, and Willkie sent word back to the President that he was willing to devote almost his full time to it because he felt "a sound liberal government in the United States is absolutely essential to continued cooperation with other nations of the world." Willkie insisted, however, that any meeting between them be held off until after the election.

The rest was hinted at more than spelled out in the letters exchanged between Willkie and Roosevelt and in the comments of others close to them. Eight days after the meeting between Willkie and Rosenman, President Roosevelt, about to start on a trip to the West, wrote Willkie that he wanted to talk to him without delay. "I want to see you when I come back, but not on anything in relationship to the present campaign. I want to talk to you about the future, even the somewhat distant future," the President wrote. "We can arrange a meeting either here in Washington or, if you prefer, at Hyde Park, wholly off the record or otherwise, just as you think best."

Willkie wrote an answer, later found in his files but never mailed because news that he might meet the President was "leaked to the press" by someone in the White House. In his unmailed letter Willkie wrote that any talk between them before the campaign was over "might well be the subject of misinterpretation and misunderstanding," and that he didn't believe they could meet privately without the fact becoming known. When the story of the possible meeting did get into the papers, instead of mailing the letter, Willkie tried to clarify the situation by having former Governor James Cox of Ohio, an old friend since his Akron days, explain his position to the President. But it was handled by Cox with such secrecy and discretion that presidential aides did not understand that Cox was representing Willkie. Meanwhile, there was additional speculation in the newspapers, and Willkie temporarily called the whole thing off.

When President Roosevelt returned from his Western trip, he sent Willkie another letter in which he asked him to please "stop in and see me in Washington or run up to Hyde Park, if you prefer." Willkie again suggested waiting until after the election. Meanwhile, he was busy writing magazine articles and considering his personal post-election plans, including the possibility that he might become publisher of a large Midwestern newspaper. One event in which he took particular pleasure was the New York premiere of a motion picture based on the life of Woodrow Wilson, which his own film company, Twentieth-Century Fox, had produced.

But the President had another reason to press for a meeting with Willkie that was even more urgent than their discussion of future political possibilities. He was considering making Willkie chief American representative in charge of political reconstruction in Europe after the final defeat of Germany. With the war rapidly moving toward victory, he wanted to sound Willkie out about it. Through other intermediaries Willkie finally agreed that he would go to Hyde Park to talk to the President as soon as possible after the Labor Day weekend.

Willkie then left for a long-postponed visit to Rushville, planning to return to New York immediately after the weekend. But his meeting with the President and all the possibilities that loomed so large in his future were never to be. On the train to Indiana, he felt a severe stab of pain when he tried to open the door of the dining car. He refused to admit to himself that it was a heart attack, but after he reached Rushville the pain became intense.

He fought against calling a doctor and told his farm manager, Mary Sleeth, that he still had too many things to do to admit to illness. Finally his condition forced him to see a doctor in Indianapolis, who advised him to enter a hospital there immediately. But he argued that if he could get back to New York perhaps he could keep the heart attack a secret. "I don't want people to think of me as just an old man with a bad heart," he said. "They'll write me off."

Willkie pledged everyone to secrecy and insisted upon boarding the train, but on his way to New York he had another attack. He had wired ahead to his aide, Lem Jones, to meet him but not to alarm Mrs. Willkie or Philip by telling them. Mary Sleeth had telephoned them, however, and they were at the station with Jones when Willkie's train arrived. He was haggard, almost helpless, but still he waited until all other passengers had left the train before he allowed himself to be helped to a taxi. He got to his New York apartment, but doctors there gave him a sedative and put him in an ambulance which took him to Lenox Hill Hospital.

A public announcement was made that he was suffering from a stomach disorder and merely needed a complete rest; the secret of his heart condition was kept from the press and denied to gossip columnists who heard rumors of it. He was in the hospital a month, and gradually did seem to regain his strength. Cheered by the fact that he had kept the nature of his illness from becoming known, he wrote to friends that he was just tired out from overwork. By the end of September, close friends who were allowed to visit him reported that he seemed to be his old self again, joking, arguing, asking more questions than they could answer. He was busily at work writing, with newspapers strewn about him and books piled on a table at his elbow, impatient for doctors to tell him how soon he could leave the hospital.

Then, on October 4, he was stricken with a streptococcic throat infection, lung congestion, and high fever. Heavy doses of penicillin pulled him through, but two days later he suffered a relapse, and the strain was too great for his weakened heart. At one o'clock in the morning of October 8, he awoke from a restful sleep and joked with his doctors and nurses, but an hour later he suffered another heart attack and was placed in an oxygen tent. At 2:20 that Sunday morning, October 8, 1944, Wendell Willkie died of coronary thrombosis.

Mrs. Willkie was at his bedside. His son Philip, on convoy duty in the Atlantic as a lieutenant in the Navy, was listening to a regular shortwave news broadcast aboard his vessel when he first learned of his father's death. Radio also spread the news across the nation, since most Sunday morning newspapers already had gone to press. In many churches, ministers put aside the sermons they had prepared and spoke instead of Wendell Willkie. Messages came by the thousands from important leaders and plain men and women around the world, and praise came from former opponents as well as from friends.

President Roosevelt, his opponent and his friend, spoke of the nation's loss of "a great citizen in this hour of greatest crisis," of a "forthright American, earnest, honest, whole-souled," and of "the tremendous courage . . . which was his dominant trait" and which "prompted him more than once to stand and challenge powerful interests." Churchill, Anthony Eden, Chiang Kai-Shek, Secretary of State Hull, and former President Hoover were among those who mourned his loss. In his unflagging search for international peace, Bernard Baruch said, Willkie's thinking was "closest to that of Woodrow Wilson."

The New York Times said in an editorial that "to have him cut down now in the full vigor of his early middle age and at a very time when he was needed most is a tragic thing," and that "a man is gone who cannot be replaced" for "his influence certainly would have been a great constructive force in dealing with the hard and dangerous problems which the postwar years seem sure to bring us." The *Times* editorial went on:

> Party, country and One World owe this man a debt which the years will not discharge. More than any other single man he fought to lead his party from isolation to cooperation on the stage of world affairs. As much as any other man he helped shape for debate and action the great issues of the most critical years in the lifetime of the American people. To the world

219

beyond our borders he was an emissary of American good will.
. . . Sorrow that his work is done will be felt wherever people cherish freedom.

The Monday morning after his death, Mrs. Willkie and his brother Edward spent a half hour alone in the Fifth Avenue Presbyterian Church where his flag-draped coffin lay. The doors were then opened to sixty thousand people who came to pay their last respects. From midday until midnight, they filed two abreast through the dimly-lighted brownstone church, some drawn merely by the desire to see him, but others weeping.

Mrs. Roosevelt represented the President at the funeral services there the next afternoon, and after former President Hoover, Governor Dewey, and other dignitaries and leaders of government, senators, congressmen, and governors were seated, the public was allowed to fill the remaining pews. But the church could hold only 2,500, and outside, filling Fifth Avenue and adjacent crosstown streets, thirty-five thousand others stood. Conducting the services, the pastor of the church, the Reverend John Sutherland Bonnell, Willkie's apartment house neighbor and longtime friend, said: "In normal times this country could ill afford to lose a citizen of his stature, but his passing now, just as the nations are approaching the crossroads which will determine whether or not the world will enjoy stability and peace or be torn by intermittent wars, takes on the aspect of tragedy."

Arlington National Cemetery had been offered for Willkie's burial, but the family decided his final resting place should be in Indiana, and his body was taken to Rushville. There, in the town where he had met his wife, and near the farms he had considered his real home, the rest of his brothers and his sister Charlotte, all his kin except for his sister Julia who had died the year before, gathered for very simple last rites that had been delayed until the arrival of his son Philip from duty at sea. Afterwards, borne by eight farmers who had been his tenants, his casket was buried on a grassy slope of Rushville's East Hill Cemetery, between two giant oaks, where his monument was an open volume carved in stone.

Through the years, thousands who remembered him would continue to come there, and on the twentieth anniversary of his death, in October, 1964, family and friends would gather again to honor his memory. There were other memorials, a community center in Des Moines, a twelve-story dormitory on the campus of Indiana University, a bronze plaque on the wall of New York's public library, and across the street from it the Willkie Memorial Building of Freedom House, headquarters for many of the organizations in which he believed, and a forum for the democratic exchange of ideas.

Newspaper columnists and political analysts soon began to speculate as to what kind of a president Wendell Willkie might have made if he had been elected. Certainly he would have been active, dynamic, ready to seek a fresh approach to problems, and to attempt new and perhaps startling solutions of them. As President, he undoubtedly would have been a leader of opinion, a man with the ability to reach and to move people. Some thought that in both international and domestic problems he would have held much the same general viewpoint as President Roosevelt. Admitting all his virtues, however, there were those who wondered whether Willkie's impulsive nature, the very bluntness of his honesty and his stubborn refusal to compromise his principles, his vision of a world too ideal to become a reality, might have worked against him as President. He was never a discreet man, not one who easily accepted expediency or had much willingness to achieve a working unity with those whose views he considered wrong.

There were others who tried to guess what changes Willkie might have brought about if he had lived on, instead of dying when he did, a month before the 1944 reelection of President Roosevelt, with the war on its way to victory but the shape of peace much in doubt. President Roosevelt's own death six months after Willkie's would have blocked any decisions they might have reached to work together to change the political parties. If Willkie had lived, his voice undoubtedly would have been raised to attack American support of anti-democratic regimes in foreign lands and to encourage the emerging new nations to seek freedom and self-government. He probably would have been a crusader in the 1950's against the red-baiting extremists of the Mc-Carthy era and certainly a battler against segregation, and for the broad application of federal power to civil rights. But what Willkie did while he lived was in relation to his own times and to transfer those actions to what was to come could be only a guessing game. Events would have shaped his decisions more than any pattern of the past.

Yet Willkie was far ahead of his time. In many things, some of his former opponents eventually concluded he was right, and many of his proposals, in social and economic fields and in civil rights, became reality years after he died. He was a great idea man, one who provided a base upon which others who followed him could work. Willkie implanted in men's minds ideas that many of them echoed long afterwards, sometimes not remembering their source, and he made America take a new look at itself and the world, produced a ferment for change that pushed public opinion in new directions. Modern travel and space exploration have made his global concept a now almost casually admitted fact of life.

The same newspapers that carried the news of Willkie's death also had headlines that agreement had been reached on the proposed charter for the United Nations organization. The United States, Britain, Russia, and China, in their conference at Dumbarton Oaks, had drafted specific proposals for founding the UN. It was far from the organization of which he had dreamed, and in its shaping and building at Yalta and San Francisco there would be many of the weaknesses he had feared and against which he had fought, so that peace would not again be lost as it had been after the First World War. Still, it was by far the greatest step the United States had ever made toward membership in a world community of nations. Others would be its architects, but he had been its prophet and had helped to clear the ground upon which it would be built.

"The time will come," Roscoe Drummond wrote in the Christian Science Monitor two days after Willkie's death, "when it can be seen that Wendell Willkie made a greater contribution to the security, the welfare, the progress and the vision of his nation than most elected presidents."

SOME OTHER BOOKS ABOUT WENDELL WILLKIE

Barnard, Ellsworth. *Wendell Willkie, Fighter for Freedom.* Northern Michigan University Press, Marquette, Michigan, 1966.

Barnes, Joseph. *Willkie.* Simon and Schuster, New York, 1952.

Hatch, Alden. *Young Willkie.* Harcourt, Brace and Company, New York, 1944.

Johnson, Donald Bruce. *The Republican Party and Wendell Willkie.* University of Illinois Press, Urbana, 1960.

Makey, Herman O. *Wendell Willkie of Elwood.* National Book Company, Elwood, Indiana, 1940.

Rukeyser, Muriel. *One Life*. Simon and Schuster, New York, 1957.

By Wendell Willkie:

This Is Wendell Willkie. Dodd, Mead and Company, New York, 1940.
One World. Simon and Schuster, New York, 1943.
An American Program. Simon and Schuster, New York, 1944.

INDEX

225

226